Soviet Military Rear Services in East Germany

Contents

Soviet Military Rear Services in East Germany

Directorate of Intelligence

Nimble Books LLC: The AI Lab for Book-Lovers

Fred Zimmerman, Editor

Humans and AI making books richer, more diverse, and more surprising

Publishing Information

- (c) 2024 Nimble Books LLC
- ISBN: 978-1-60888-330-1

Nimble Books LLC ~ NimbleBooks.com

Bibliographic Key Phrases

Soviet military logistics; East Germany; Warsaw Pact; Group of Soviet Forces, Germany (GSFG); Theater of Military Operations (TMO); ammunition; petroleum, oil, and lubricants (POL); force reconstitution; medical support; technical support; rail transport; motor transport; lines of communication; boyevoy komplekt; boyekomplekt;

Publisher's Note

The Cold War may be over, but the world remains a dangerous place. This is why it is essential to understand the military capabilities of potential adversaries. This Cold War-era document is a rare glimpse into the vast and powerful Soviet military logistics system as it was prepared to fight NATO in the 1980s. This research paper, compiled by the CIA"s Directorate of Intelligence, provides a detailed overview of Soviet military rear services in East Germany, covering everything from ammunition stockpiles and fuel distribution networks to battlefield medical care and equipment repair. The paper, based on an exhaustive review of Soviet and Warsaw Pact writings, satellite imagery, and interviews with former military personnel, reveals the Soviets' extensive and carefully planned logistic preparations. The document details how the Soviets planned to support a major war in Europe, including the movement of troops and supplies, the treatment of casualties, and the repair of damaged equipment. It also provides a fascinating glimpse into the Soviets' doctrine and planning processes for artillery fire and the use of the "boyevoy komplekt" (BK) unit. This document is a must-read for anyone interested in understanding the Cold War, the military history of the Soviet Union, or the complexities of military logistics in a modern warfare setting.

This annotated edition illustrates the capabilities of the AI Lab for Book-Lovers to add context and ease-of-use to manuscripts. It includes publishing information; abstracts; viewpoints; learning aids; and references.

Abstracts

TLDR (three words)

Soviet logistics are ready.

ELI5

This is a report written by spies about the Soviet army's plan to fight a war against a group of countries called NATO. The spies are trying to figure out how the Soviet army plans to bring all of their stuff, like food, bullets, and tanks, to where they need to be when they are fighting. The spies are worried because they think the Soviet army could bring a lot of tanks to fight against NATO in a very short time.

Scientific-Style Abstract

This research paper examines Soviet military rear services in East Germany. The paper, based on a review of Soviet and Warsaw Pact doctrine, imagery analysis, and the author's knowledge of Soviet military practice, concludes that the Soviets have established sufficient logistical capabilities to support at least two fronts in a major war in Central Europe. Since the early 1970s, the Soviets have been methodically expanding these capabilities, making it more difficult to detect a Soviet buildup by observing logistic preparations. The paper's findings suggest that the Soviets now have the option of moving combat troops rather than material into Central Europe early in a war, as soon as they can be dispatched from the western USSR.

Learning Aids

Mnemonic (acronym)

SPARTANS

Stockpiles **POL** **A**mmunition **R**econstuction **T**ransport **A**rtillery **N**uclear **S**upport

Mnemonic (speakable)

Soviet troops rely on stockpiles, POL, and ammunition, plus a strong ability to reconstruct, transport, and support a war with a nuclear punch.

Mnemonic (singable)

To the tune of "My Bonnie"

Oh, the Soviets have their plans To fight a war, they know their stance In East Germany, their war reserve Stockpiles abound, they'll persevere

POL, ammo, they've got it all To wage a war, to stand tall Trucks and trains, they'll use them well And if they have to, they'll give hell

Oh, the Soviets have their plans To fight a war, they know their stance In East Germany, their war reserve Stockpiles abound, they'll persevere

Soviet logistics, a mighty force Rear services, they'll take their course To win a war, they'll do their best In East Germany, they'll put the test

Oh, the Soviets have their plans To fight a war, they know their stance In East Germany, their war reserve Stockpiles abound, they'll persevere

Excerpts

Most Important Passages

Soviet logistic preparations in East Germany are much greater than earlier estimates have indicated. An exhaustive review of Soviet logistic facilities as of January 1984 confirms that currently available rear services organizations, equipment, and depot stocks of ammunition and fuel are adequate to support at least twice as many Soviet forces as are currently located in East Germany. (p. 3)

The Soviets in East Germany have fuel storage facilities with a capacity to hold more than 600,000 metric tons. In the initial period of a war, they would take control of East German national reserves and the fuel in the main "Friendship" pipelines from the USSR into Central Europe. These resources, combined with Soviet military stocks, probably would fulfill the Soviets' 90-day war reserve requirements for two fronts. (p. 3)

The Soviets in East Germany have established an extensive capability to repair and rebuild their damaged military equipment, and they have pre-positioned the equipment for mobile maintenance units in amounts adequate for the support of at least two fronts. The lift capacity of Soviet military trucks currently in East Germany already far exceeds the doctrinal transport requirements for a single front, and these probably are to be supplemented by East German trucks, military and civilian. (p. 3)

The logistic buildup lagged nearly a decade behind the buildup of combat forces and weapon systems, creating for a time the impression that the Soviets did not plan to maintain a substantial logistic capability in peacetime. That impression has been erased by the steady expansion of logistics over the past decade. For example: - Since 1977, the capacity of ammunition depots has nearly doubled. - Since the early 1970s, equipment pre-positioned for mobile medical and maintenance units has doubled. - Since 1978, the introduction of Kamaz trucks has increased the lift capacity of active nondivisional motor transport units by about 60 percent. (p. 4)

We believe the Soviets intend much of this logistic buildup-which appears to greatly exceed the doctrinal requirement for their forces now in East Germany-as a reserve for the Western Theater of Military Operations, especially forces we believe would attack NATO in southern West Germany. These pre-positioned logistics would give them the option of reinforcing East Germany with combat troops coming from the USSR rather than clogging lines of communication with materiel supply trains. The logistic manpower and materials already in place in East Germany probably make the Soviet planners confident that they could sustain the initial period of a war. In order to support a prolonged war, however, the Soviets would have to mobilize large numbers of support personnel and send them from the USSR to fill out the logistic formations. (p. 4)

During the past decade the Soviets have so methodically and thoroughly improved their capability to support forces in East Germany that logistic buildups, which once might have been key indicators of impending military operations, now probably have little potential to provide such warning. Furthermore, the Soviets now have the option of moving combat troops instead of supplies to Central Europe early in the war, as soon as they can be dispatched from the western USSR. (p. 4)

According to Soviet writings, the acquisition, handling, and distribution of petroleum, oil, and lubricants (POL) for Soviet ground forces is the responsibility of the Fuels Supply Service. Each echelon has a fuels supply officer who is in charge of POL-associated personnel and operations. He is subordinate to the deputy commander for rear services. (p. 19)

References

Glossary

This glossary defines technical terms from the research paper "Soviet Military Rear Services in East Germany" that might be unfamiliar to a lay reader.

- **Boyekomplekt (BK)**: A standard unit of measurement used by Soviet military planners to calculate ammunition requirements for specific weapons and military units. It is also called boyevoy komplekt. For example, the BK for a 152mm howitzer might be 60 rounds.
- **Combined Armed Forces (CAF)**: The unified command structure of the Warsaw Pact, with a headquarters staff dominated by the Soviet Union. It is responsible for coordinating the military activities of all Warsaw Pact members during a war.
- **Conservation**: The practice of storing military equipment for long periods of time to minimize wear and tear. The equipment is typically given regular preventive maintenance and inspections to ensure its reliability when needed.
- **Front**: In Soviet and Warsaw Pact military doctrine, a large military formation typically comprising three to five armies and one or more air forces. A front would be responsible for a particular theater of operations and could range from 300,000 to 400,000 men.
- **Group of Soviet Forces, Germany (GSFG)**: The Soviet military force stationed in East Germany. It was a major component of the Warsaw Pact and was responsible for defending the Soviet Union's western border.
- **Lines of Communication (LOCs)**: The routes and infrastructure used to transport troops, supplies, and equipment in a military operation.

- **Materiel**: The equipment and supplies used by the military.
- **Military District**: A Soviet administrative region encompassing several military units and their logistical support units.
- **Military Motor Road**: A road specifically designated for military use. These roads have been constructed and maintained to handle the heavy traffic of military vehicles.
- **Non-Soviet Warsaw Pact (NSWP)**: The Warsaw Pact members other than the Soviet Union.
- **Petroleum, Oil, and Lubricants (POL)**: The fuel and lubricants used by the military.
- **Pre-positioned**: Military equipment and supplies that are stored in advance in a particular location for use during a war.
- **Provisional**: Temporary units or formations that are formed in wartime to supplement regular units and meet specific military needs.
- **Rear Services**: The military units and support functions that are responsible for logistics. Rear services include transportation, supply, maintenance, medical care, and other support activities.

- **Triage**: A system for classifying casualties based on the severity of their injuries. Casualties are sorted into categories based on the urgency of their medical needs, with the most serious cases being treated first.
- **TMO**: Theater of Military Operations, in Warsaw Pact military doctrine, a large geographical area where military operations are to be conducted.
- **Untouchable Reserve (NZ)**: A military stockpile of critical supplies that is not to be used for routine operations. The NZ is intended for emergencies and is only to be accessed with the consent of a high-ranking commander.
- **Warsaw Pact**: A military alliance of Soviet-bloc countries formed in 1955 as a counterweight to NATO.

This glossary provides a foundation for understanding the terms you will encounter in this research paper.

Timeline

June, 1941: The German military invades the Soviet Union.

December, 1941: The Soviet Union reorganizes its logistic system.

February, 1980: Nine Soviet ammunition storage depots are under expansion in East Germany, and seven new ones are under construction.

February, 1980: Soviet tanks in East Germany are loaded with ammunition in peacetime.

Early, 1984: Construction of the expanded and new ammunition storage depots in East Germany is projected to be completed.

Early, 1970s: The Soviet military introduces field refueling points.

Mid-1960s: Soviet artillery planners experience problems estimating conventional ammunition requirements.

Mid-1960s: One Soviet military author estimates that 230,000 to 270,000 metric tons of fuel would be required for a front operation to a depth of 2,000 km. Another author estimates 180,000 metric tons would be required for a front operation to a depth of 1,000 km.

Mid-1960s: A Soviet author estimates that 400,000 to 450,000 metric tons of supplies would be required for a front operation to a depth of about 2,000 km.

Mid-1960s: Participants in Soviet military exercises begin with quantities of ammunition specified by the scenario authors, and then negotiate lower ones.

Mid-1960s: Soviet military doctrine specifies that 120,000 to 150,000 metric tons of conventional ammunition would be required for a front operation to a depth of 1,000 km.

Mid-1960s: Soviet artillery planners emphasize the use of nuclear weapons in military exercises.

Late 1950s: Soviet military units begin to receive nuclear weapons.

Late 1960s: Soviet military doctrine estimates that 250,000 to 300,000 metric tons of fuel would be required for a front operation to a depth of 1,000 km.

Late 1960s: The Soviets replace older ZIL and Gaz trucks with Ural models.

Late 1960s: One Soviet military author estimates that each launcher in a front operation would be allocated three rounds, two nuclear and one chemical.

Late 1960s: A Soviet military author indicates that the amount of ammunition required for a 1,000-km front operation was approximately 80,000 metric tons.

Late 1960s: Soviet military doctrine specifies that ammunition be stored at various locations in the military hierarchy.

Late 1970s: The Soviets replace Ural trucks with Kamaz models.

Late 1970s: Soviet military doctrine indicates that a front might have 130 to 160 rockets and missiles.

Late 1970s: British tour officers discover a stepdown valve in East Germany with which tactical pipe could be coupled to the main pipeline.

Late 1970s: The Soviets begin to stockpile ammunition for Theater of Military Operations (TMO) war reserves.

Late 1970s: Soviet military doctrine estimates that 300 to 400 nuclear missiles or rockets would be used during a front operation.

1972: Mobile medical equipment is stored at 27 Soviet military hospitals in East Germany.

1973: The Ural truck-plus-trailer became the primary vehicle observed in motor transport units of the Group of Soviet Forces Germany (GSFG).

1974: Seven Soviet POL storage depots in East Germany were constructed.

1976: The GSFG has about 185,000 metric tons of ammunition storage capacity.

1977: Soviet military doctrine specifies that each front should have two or three axial railroads and two or three laterals, each line able to handle 60 to 70 trains per day in each direction.

1977: Soviet military doctrine estimates that about 160 to 180 nuclear missiles or rockets would be used during the initial nuclear strike of a front operation.

1977: The Soviets begin replacing Ural trucks with Kamaz models in the GSFG.

1977: The capacity of ammunition depots in East Germany nearly doubles.

1977: A transshipment and distribution facility is constructed at Rostock.

1978: The Soviets begin storing large numbers of trucks at several maintenance facilities in the GSFG.

1978: The Soviets reorganize the Warsaw Pact Combined Armed Forces (CAF).

1980: Soviet military doctrine estimates that 8,000 to 10,000 vehicles per day could traverse front roads, but army road requirements remain unchanged.

1980: The Soviets begin constructing regiment-size equipment sets at armored vehicle, wheeled vehicle, and artillery maintenance facilities in East Germany.

1982: The GSFG has a third Scud brigade disbanded, and its equipment is combined with the other two.

1982: The Soviets increase their pre-positioning of mobile medical equipment sets in East Germany.

January, 1984: An exhaustive review of Soviet logistic facilities in East Germany is conducted, confirming that currently available rear services organizations, equipment, and depot stocks of ammunition and fuel are adequate to support at least twice as many Soviet forces as are currently located in East Germany.

July, 1978: The work *Soviet Armed Forces Rear Services in the Great Patriotic War of 1941-1945* is translated into English.

Index of Places

Index of Technologies

Index of Soviet Military Doctrine

Index of Logistic Support Units

25X1

**Directorate of
Intelligence**

Top Secret

Soviet Military Rear Services
in East Germany

25X1

A Research Paper

Top Secret

*SOV 84-10006JX
IA 84-10012 IX*

February 1984

25X1

Copy 3 3 0

**Directorate of
Intelligence**

Top Secret

25X1

25X1

Soviet Military Rear Services in East Germany

25X1

A Research Paper

This paper was prepared by [   ] Office 25X1
of Soviet Analysis, [   ] Office of 25X1
Imagery Analysis. [   ] 25X1
[   ] Conventional Forces Division, Office of 25X1
Imagery Analysis, contributed to its preparation.

25X1

Comments and queries are welcome and may be
directed to the Chief, Theater Forces Division,
SOVA [   ] or to the Chief, Conventional 25X1
Forces Division, OIA, [   ] 25X1

Top Secret 25X1
SOV 84-10006JX
IA 84-10012JX

February 1984 25X1

Top Secret

━━ 25X1

Soviet Military Rear Services
in East Germany [ ]

━ ━ ━ ━ ━ ━ ━ ━ 25X1

Summary

*Information available
as of 1 January 1984
was used in this report.*

Soviet logistic preparations in East Germany are much greater than earlier estimates have indicated. An exhaustive review of Soviet logistic facilities confirms that currently available rear services organizations, equipment, and depot stocks of ammunition and fuel are adequate to support at least twice as many Soviet forces as are currently located in East Germany. ┐ - - 25X1

 25X1

 On the basis of 25X1

Soviet doctrinal writings, we judge that this is a stockpile adequate to satisfy 90-day war reserve requirements for about two fronts. ┐ - - - 25X1
└ - - - - - - - - - - - - - - - - - - - 25X1

The Soviets in East Germany have fuel storage facilities with a capacity to hold more than 600,000 metric tons. In the initial period of a war, they would take control of East German national reserves and the fuel in the main "Friendship" pipelines from the USSR into Central Europe. These resources, combined with Soviet military stocks, probably would fulfill the Soviets' 90-day war reserve requirements for two fronts. ┐ - - - 25X1

Soviet military hospitals in East Germany appear to have enough beds, according to Soviet norms, to treat casualties for one front for about 30 days of combat, or up to about three fronts in the initial period of a war. In addition, some garrison buildings are likely to be used as hospitals after the combat troops have left them, and the East Germans probably are to provide additional hospital beds. Supplemented in this way, the military medical establishment in East Germany almost certainly is capable of satisfying Soviet medical requirements for more than one front. ┐ - - - 25X1

The Soviets in East Germany have established an extensive capability to repair and rebuild their damaged military equipment, and they have pre-positioned the equipment for mobile maintenance units in amounts adequate for the support of at least two fronts. The lift capacity of Soviet military trucks currently in East Germany already far exceeds the doctrinal transport requirements for a single front, and these probably are to be supplemented by East German trucks, military and civilian. ┐ - - - 25X1

The logistic buildup lagged nearly a decade behind the buildup of combat forces and weapon systems, creating for a time the impression that the Soviets did not plan to maintain a substantial logistic capability in

 - - - - - - - - iii - - - - - - - - - -
Top Secret

SOV 84-10006JX
IA 84-10012JX

February 1984
━ ━ ━ 25X1

━ 25X1

Body-4

25X1

peacetime. That impression has been erased by the steady expansion of logistics over the past decade. For example:

- Since 1977, the capacity of ammunition depots has nearly doubled.
- Since the early 1970s, equipment pre-positioned for mobile medical and maintenance units has doubled.
- Since 1978, the introduction of Kamaz trucks has increased the lift capacity of active nondivisional motor transport units by about 60 percent.

25X1

We believe the Soviets intend much of this logistic buildup—which appears to greatly exceed the doctrinal requirement for their forces now in East Germany—as a reserve for the Western Theater of Military Operations, especially forces we believe would attack NATO in southern West Germany. These pre-positioned logistics would give them the option of reinforcing East Germany with combat troops coming from the USSR rather than clogging lines of communication with materiel supply trains. The logistic manpower and materials already in place in East Germany probably make the Soviet planners confident that they could sustain the initial period of a war. In order to support a prolonged war, however, the Soviets would have to mobilize large numbers of support personnel and send them from the USSR to fill out the logistic formations.

25X1

During the past decade the Soviets have so methodically and thoroughly improved their capability to support forces in East Germany that logistic buildups, which once might have been key indicators of impending military operations, now probably have little potential to provide such warning. Furthermore, the Soviets now have the option of moving combat troops instead of supplies to Central Europe early in the war, as soon as they can be dispatched from the western USSR.

25X1

iv

25X1
25X1

25X1

Contents

25X1

25X1

25X1
25X1

Top Secret

25X1

Appendixes

25X1

Figures

25X1

Top Secret

vi

25X1
25X1

25X1

Soviet Military Rear Services in East Germany

25X1

Background

The Soviets' approach to military logistics is strongly influenced by history and geography. According to a Soviet military historian, experience in World War I, the Civil War, and their war with Finland, plus observation of the Spanish Civil War, led the Soviets to believe on the eve of the Great Patriotic War (World War II) that some time would pass from the declaration of war until the beginning of military operations. Consequently, they maintained only a minimum of rear services organizations during peacetime, but planned to activate an extensive logistic organization during mobilization and establish a network of fixed bases.

25X1

The Soviet logistic bureaucracy in the late 1930s was ill organized. Supplies were controlled by a chief of arms and services directly subordinate to the commander at each echelon of service. Rail and air transportation was provided by the Soviet Army Military Lines of Communications Directorate, subordinate to the Chief of the General Staff. Trucking was organized by motor road service departments in the rear services sections of military districts and army staffs. In each major component, a deputy chief of staff for rear services organized the rear zone and planned the receipt of supplies and their delivery to combat units.

25X1

Under these conditions, the Soviets were totally unprepared for the German onslaught of June 1941. During the ensuing 18 months they reorganized their logistic system completely, and by 1944 it was able to support large-scale offensive operations. We believe the Soviets have resolved never again to allow such a situation to arise.[1]

25X1

[1] For a detailed description of Soviet logistic activities during World War II, see *Tyl Sovetskiky Vooruzhennykh Sil v Velikoy Otechestvennoy Voyne 1941-1945 gg*, ed. S. K. Kurkotkin, Moscow: Voyenizdat, 1977. This work has been translated as *Soviet Armed Forces Rear Services in the Great Patriotic War of 1941-1945*, JPRS L/7875, 7 July 1978.

25X1

Geography also influences Soviet planning. In a war with NATO, Soviet troops would fight in Central Europe, separated from the USSR by the territory of their Warsaw Pact allies. Men and equipment would have to move long distances, relying on their allies for transit rights and for the security of their lines of communication (LOCs).

25X1

Warsaw Pact Cooperation

The Combined Armed Forces

The legal foundations for a unified Warsaw Pact command already exist. Warsaw Pact writings indicate that during peacetime a High Command of the Combined Armed Forces (CAF) guides the member states' military activities. The CAF staff is dominated by the Soviets, who mold the other members' forces and doctrine after their own. The CAF is funded by contributions from member states and levies requirements for men and equipment that are to be subordinate to Warsaw Pact command during a war. Logistic planning is organized by a CAF deputy commander for rear services and his staff.

25X1

25X1

The Theaters of Military Operations

High commands will be established in wartime to control forces in the Western and Southwestern Theaters of Military Operations (TMOs). The theater commands will be subordinate to the Warsaw Pact Supreme High Command (which is the Soviet Supreme High Command) and to a Soviet Supreme Commander.[2] The officers who are to fill TMO staff positions are designated in peacetime: the peacetime

25X1

[2] During his lifetime, Leonid Brezhnev was the Supreme Commander-designate.

25X1

25X1

25X1
25X1

25X1

CAF Commander in Chief will command the Western TMO, and his deputy will command the Southwestern TMO. We believe the transformation of the CAF into two TMO commands will take place similarly throughout the entire staff. Thus, the deputy CAF commander for rear services will be deputy commander of the Western TMO for rear services and his deputy will be the deputy commander of the Southwestern TMO for rear services.[3]

Warsaw Pact writings indicate that uniform principles for support of Pact combat operations have been in force at least since the late 1960s. These are general guidelines for the organization and operation of support systems and were established through a series of agreements. In general, each Warsaw Pact nation is to support its own combat forces. If forces are resubordinated for an operation, either of the two nations may provide support, under the condition that supplies issued for the multinational formation be repaid by monetary transfer or barter agreement. Warsaw Pact nations are required to allocate supplies to the CAF to establish TMO reserves and to develop, maintain, and restore lines of communication, which are specified by agreement with the CAF. Finally, administrative procedures have been developed to standardize such things as requisition requirements, procedures, and even language (Russian) to facilitate joint operations during a war.[4]

Materiel support of Soviet combat units is provided by the military's rear services. Rear services units:
- Transport all types of supplies from depots and mobile bases to military consumers.
- Repair and evacuate damaged or malfunctioning equipment and maintain stocks of spare parts.
- Collect and evacuate personnel casualties and provide sanitation and preventive medical services.
- Maintain and repair lines of communication.
- Organize the exploitation of captured stocks and equipment.
- Provide security for rear areas.

[4] Non-Soviet Warsaw Pact (NSWP) allies cannot always meet these many demands. One NSWP country, for example, has resisted CAF pressures to increase military stockpiles and improve lines of communications because it could not afford to allocate the large amounts of resources that those improvements would require.

According to Soviet writings of the 1960s and early 1970s, the front support structure was to be the link connecting support echelons in the USSR with the rear zone of operating armies.[5] Once the front was activated, its logistic apparatus would undertake the above rear service responsibilities, on the larger scale.

25X1

More recent Pact writings indicate, however, that the CAF was reorganized in 1978, and wartime command structures were formed for its two TMOs. We believe one effect of this peacetime institutionalization of a structure designed for war was the insertion of an additional level of command—the TMO—between the USSR and the fronts in Eastern Europe. This would also institutionalize an associated TMO logistic apparatus.

25X1

25X1

Organization of Rear Services

According to Soviet writings, there is no standard structure for the rear services of a front or an army. Instead, ad hoc support organizations are to be tailored to suit the specific requirements of a particular combat mission and organization. In wartime, the logistic elements subordinate to a front could comprise several hundred units and 160,000 to 170,000 men, and the logistic apparatus of an army could include 30 to 50 units and some 7,000 men. In peacetime, however, a front's rear services organizations overall are to be manned at only 30 to 40 percent of their wartime manpower authorizations, and an army's rear units should have 45 to 50 percent.

25X1
25X1

[5] Although not directly comparable to any Western organization, a Warsaw Pact front in wartime would be similar to a NATO army group and its associated air forces in size, level of command, and function. There is no standard organization for a front. It usually would be composed of three to five ground armies (each including three to five tank or motorized rifle divisions) and one or more air forces (each including several hundred tactical aircraft). The overall size of a typical front depends on the mission assigned and probably would range from 300,000 to 400,000 men. According to US National Intelligence Estimates, the Soviet–East German Front could total more than 500,000 men after full mobilization.

25X1
25X1
25X1

25X1

25X1
25X1

2

25X1

25X1

Although personnel levels are below wartime require-ments in peacetime for logistic units, materiel stocks are another matter altogether. Soviet writings consist-ently advocate stocking 20 to 25 days' supplies in a front.[6] Of these, stocks for three to five days of combat are to be kept by divisions, for two days by armies, and for 13 to 15 days by front supply bases. In addition, stocks for about three months of war are to be positioned in peacetime in areas where they are most likely to be needed in war; these are to be dispersed to minimize the potential for their destruc-tion by nuclear attack.

25X1

Materiel enters a front's area via its rear zone. Soviet writings indicate that the front's rear zone can be 300 to 400 km deep in peacetime and may extend to nearly 1,000 km during a combat operation. In peace-time, supplies apparently are delivered to a relatively few fixed depots and installations. During wartime, however, the Soviets intend to establish a series of supply bases for moving supplies to the combat divi-sions.

A front's rear supply bases are located deep in its rear area along major rail routes. Within a rear area 3,000 to 5,000 km square, the front maintains supply depots, hospitals, repair facilities, motor transport units, and other support organizations. These entities:

- Maintain around 60 to 70 percent of front materiel reserves (enough for about 10 days of combat).
- Provide for the transport of materiel toward the battle zone.
- Issue supplies to second-echelon troops, reserves, and other units stationed deep in the front's rear area

Each front rear supply base can detach two branches, whose composition apparently is dictated by the tacti-cal situation. We suspect that these branches may be deployed within the rear area, either laterally to

reduce congestion along lines of communications or forward to establish an intermediate distribution point between the front's rear and forward supply bases.

25X1

A front's forward supply bases, like the rear bases, contain supply depots, hospitals, repair facilities, and motor transport units, but they maintain reserves for only three or four days of combat operations. These facilities usually are dispersed near major roads with-in an area of about 150 square kilometers. Some may be mobile.

25X1

25X1

Each forward supply base can detach one branch. One Soviet author noted in the mid-1960s that the front forward supply base—and possibly its branches— would be located on the national boundary

25X1

25X1

Army mobile supply bases are designed to maintain reserves of basic supplies sufficient for about two days of combat operations. They consist largely of truck-borne supply points, and they are kept small for mobility and flexibility on the battlefield.

25X1

25X1

25X1

Figure 1 illustrates the way in which the rear services supply organization is to change in response to chang-ing combat situations.

25X1

The units that operate these supply bases are being reorganized. In the late 1960s, Soviet military authors noted an organizational problem: large quantities of supplies were to be stored on trucks, but the motor transport unit commanders responsible for the trucks were not legally responsible for the materiel on them. To solve it, the Soviets have developed a new organi-zation, the materiel support unit, in which both the depot and the motor transport unit are under one commander—one legally accountable authority. We suspect that this new name has been given to front forward supply bases, army mobile supply bases, and divisional resupply elements alike.

25X1

25X1

25X1

25X1

[6] During a war, a front is to execute initial and subsequent operations as part of a strategic operation in a TMO. In the Western TMO we believe a front would be expected to carry out an initial nuclear or nonnuclear operation to a depth of 600 to 800 km over a period of 12 to 15 days.

25X1

As illustrated in figure 1, the network of supply bases is to expand like an accordian during a front operation. Actual deployment patterns probably will vary depending on the number of bases assigned to a front, but in general the supply lines will be extended as tactical formations advance:

- A front's rear supply bases are to support the armies subordinate to the front for a few days in the initial period of war, or as long as the armies are within 200 to 250 km. At that distance, the front establishes forward supply bases.

- A front's forward supply bases resupply the armies—probably daily—and are in turn replenished from the rear supply bases every two or three days. When the armies have advanced about another 150 km, a forward supply base can either redeploy or establish a branch closer to the army.

- During combat, a front's rear supply base can establish one or two branches. These branches can be at alternate railheads to augment the rear supply base itself, or they can be at intermediate points between the rear and forward supply bases of the front.

- Each army's mobile supply base stays within 40 to 60 km of the combat divisions, to provide them with basic supplies daily. These bases are to move forward whenever the distance to the division rear becomes about 120 km, or about every other day.[7]

Key Soviet Logistic Concerns

This paper is based on information from all available sources, which include Soviet and Warsaw Pact unclassified and classified military writings, satellite imagery,

Analysis of

[7] Distances noted above are based on the Soviet norms for one day of travel by a truck with a single driver (250 to 300 km). These distances could double if the Soviets were to assign a two-man crew to each truck. For daily resupply, the Soviets require distances short enough to make a round trip in one day. Less frequent resupply permits layovers and consequently can involve greater distances.

the information indicates that the Soviets are most concerned that their logistic system shall:
- Assure the availability of adequate stocks of critical supplies.
- Reconstitute forces rapidly by treating casualties and repairing damaged equipment.
- Provide a transportation network that can move supplies forward and casualties to the rear during a war.

The sections that follow treat these key concerns in detail.

25X1

Stockpiles of Critical Supplies

Our analysis of Soviet and Warsaw Pact writings indicates that the Soviets have established methods for estimating wartime requirements of all types of supplies and norms for stockpiling them all. It is also clear that they consider the most important items to be ammunition, POL (petroleum, oil, and lubricants), and rations—in that order. The Soviets intend to have on hand in peacetime enough stocks for two to three months of combat (they believe industry would need about that much time to convert from peacetime to wartime production levels). Within each front, they intend to maintain enough supplies to sustain an entire front operation—which, at least through the mid-1970s, they anticipated would last about two weeks.

25X1

During the 1960s and 1970s the Soviets increased their estimates of the total amount of supplies required for an operation. One author estimated in 1964 that some 400,000 to 450,000 metric tons of all supplies would be required for a front operation to a depth of about 2,000 km (Paris is about 800 km from Berlin). In 1969, however, another author estimated that more than 500,000 metric tons would be necessary for an operation of about 1,000 km, and by 1977 a third estimated 500,000 to 700,000 metric tons for a 1,000-km operation. Our analysis of these and other writings suggests that these increases may have been caused by Soviet perceptions that a future war might not be nuclear, at least at its outset, and conventional operations might last longer and use more supplies.

25X1

25X1

25X1

25X1

25X1

0-14

For most categories of supplies, we cannot estimate how much the Soviets have stockpiled. This is because most items (uniforms, blankets, and rations, for example) are small enough to be stored in warehouses in quantities we cannot determine. To estimate the general degree to which the Soviets have accumulated supplies in East Germany, therefore, we examined their potential to stock two categories of supplies that can be determined—ammunition and POL. Even for these, however, we can estimate only overall storage capacity; we cannot determine the mix of ammunition and POL in storage areas

25X1

Ammunition

In both peace and war, each front and army head-quarters prepares an estimate of its ammunition requirements. At each headquarters at least three separate components work together on the task. Classified Soviet writings indicate that:

- The front (or army) operations directorate prepares the overall front (or army) training and operations (battle) plans, for which the front (or army) commander of rocket troops and artillery has prepared the artillery portion.

- On the basis of the overall plan, the front (or army) chief of rocket and artillery armament and his staff—subordinate to the deputy front (or army) commander of armament and equipment—estimate the ammunition required and arrange for its issuance.

- The transportation of ammunition from depots to troop units is arranged by a transport services group, which is subordinate to the deputy front (or army) commander for rear services.

Conventional Ammunition
The amount of ammunition maintained in ammunition stockpiles probably is based on training and operations plans. Soviet writings indicate that these stocks are divided into two general categories: current stocks and an untouchable reserve (*neprikosnovennom zapasa*, NZ). We believe that during peacetime the current stocks are the ammunition required for training and the NZ is a reserve for war. During wartime,

current stocks are those required for combat operations, and the small untouchable reserve is for use only in emergencies and with the consent of the next higher commander.[8] Soviet writings describing requirements for supplies in general suggest that war-time current ammunition stocks probably include ammunition required for (1) the preparation and conduct of the initial operation, (2) subsequent operations, and (3) replacement of ammunition lost in combat—calculated at 25 to 30 percent of total current stocks.

25X1
25X1

We have various writings indicating the way to determine the amount of ammunition to put into these stockpiles. It applies theoretical "operational-tactical" and "organizational-technical" considerations to specific operations and training plans to derive the amount of ammunition these plans require.[9] We have not attempted to replicate this process; indeed, there are indications that the Soviets themselves have had problems with it.[10]

25X1

Classified writings of the mid-1960s indicate that after the late 1950s, when Soviet units began to receive nuclear weapons, fire planners concentrated almost exclusively on the conduct of nuclear warfare. In exercises, for example, participants were criticized for errors in the use of nuclear weapons or for failures to allocate fuel correctly, but not for errors in the allocation and distribution of conventional ammunition. By the mid-1960s, Soviet artillery planners

---

[8] Our definition of "wartime current stocks" is based on published NSWP military doctrine. Because NSWP countries use training manuals written by the Soviets, we believe that this definition probably applies to Soviet forces as well.
25X1
[9] Theoretical considerations of Soviet artillery fire planning are described in appendix A.
25X1
[10] In the past, we estimated Soviet ammunition requirements on the basis of "standard" division, army, and front structures, even though Soviet armies and fronts are not standard but are to be tailored to specific circumstances. Theoretically, at least, it may soon be possible for us to apply the Soviets' system to estimate ammunition requirements for specific formations: estimates of the number and type of weapons in a division, army, or front (as noted in the US Intelligence Community's Land Arms and Manpower Model—LAMM—data base) will be combined with ammunition allocation norms or practices noted in exercises to provide—at least in general terms—the amount of ammunition the Soviets believe would be required for specific military tasks.
25X1

25X1

allegedly had forgotten how to estimate their conventional ammunition requirements properly, and authors were not sure their existing artillery norms would be applicable to a modern battlefield. (The artillery norms used in exercises usually were furnished to a unit by the umpires and were drawn from World War II experience.) Artillery theoreticians noted that because of serious supply problems during World War II, that war's consumption rates had been lower than those specified by the 1940s targeting norms, and they questioned whether norms based on that consumption rate would be adequate for the newer operational tasks.

25X1

According to the writings we have examined, participants in exercises of the early 1960s rarely calculated the amount of ammunition required for a given scenario. Instead, they began with quantities specified by the scenario's authors, then negotiated lower ones, alleging that they could not resupply the quantities specified by the umpires. For all these reasons, the authors called for exercises conducted specifically to revalidate ammunition allocation norms, anticipating that amounts required in a modern war probably would turn out to be higher than was being planned.

Soviet authorities apparently responded to these criticisms. Two contrasting estimates of the amount of ammunition required for a front operation are available from about the time the articles cited above were published. Exercises of the mid-1960s suggested to Soviet authors in one case that about 115,000 to 125,000 metric tons of ammunition would be required for a front operation to a depth of some 2,000 km, and, in another, that 80,000 metric tons would be needed for a front operation to a depth of 1,000 km. We conclude that during the period the Soviets believed a 1,000-km front operation would require some 60,000 to 80,000 metric tons of ammunition. During the late 1960s and mid-1970s, however, written Soviet doctrine specified that 120,000 to 150,000 metric tons would be required for a front operation to a depth of 1,000 km—nearly twice the earlier estimate. In addition, Soviet estimates of the number of units of fire required for a front operation under nuclear and conventional conditions more than doubled during the same period (table 1).

As noted in the section on Organization of Rear Services, however, the Soviet discussions of pre-positioning ammunition are in terms of months of combat, not of front operations. We used published Soviet norms for the calculation of reserves for the first three months of a war to estimate the peacetime stockpile requirements for a front. The calculations indicate that front stocks should amount to around 300,000 to 400,000 metric tons.

25X1

Finally, Soviet writings specify that ammunition be stored at locations controlled by various levels in the military hierarchy. As of the mid-1970s, ammunition for ground forces was to be stored in wartime as illustrated in table 2.[11] These data suggest that about half of a front's ammunition is to be stored in depots subordinate to the front, about one-tenth in army supply bases, and about one-third in division and regiment trains. Distributing in this way the 300,000 to 400,000 tons of ammunition that a front might stockpile in peacetime, we judge that 150,000 to 200,000 metric tons would be stored at front depots, 15,000 to 20,000 metric tons in each army's depots, and some 100,000 to 130,000 metric tons in division and regiment areas.

25X1

25X1

25X1

Conventional Ammunition Stocks in East Germany

Estimates of Soviet storage practices and the size of storage sheds suggest that some 700,000 metric tons of Soviet ammunition could be stored in East Germany. These stocks are dispersed among many depots, which probably are subordinate to at least three different levels of command—tactical units, armies, and the Group of Soviet Forces, Germany (GSFG)—and possibly to the TMO. Figure 2 shows the distribution of the front- and army-level depots.

25X1

25X1

. In 1977 the Soviets began to build new

25X1

[11] We have no information concerning the peacetime control of ammunition stockpiles. We suspect that they are very similar to wartime specifications, however, because the Soviets attach high importance to preparing in peacetime for wartime logistic requirements

25X1

25X1

8

25X1

Table 1
Units of Fire Required for a Front Operation [a]

Type of Ammunition	Mid-1960s		Mid-1970s	
	Nuclear	Conventional	Nuclear	Conventional
Small arms	1.0	3.0	3.5 to 4.0	4.0 to 4.5
Artillery	2.0	4.5	5.0 to 5.5	7.5 to 9.0
Tank	1.5	4.5	6.5 to 7.5	7.5 to 8.0
Antiaircraft	2.0	4.5	8.5 to 9.5	8.5 to 9.5

[a] A unit of fire (*boyevoy komplekt*, BK) is a quantity of ammunition that is separately defined for each gun or weapon system and military unit. It serves as a supply calculation unit for estimating ammunition requirements and for planning ammunition transport. Thus, for example, in the mid-1960s the Soviets would have allocated 270 conventional rounds per 152-mm howitzer during a nonnuclear front operation, but by the mid-1970s this allocation had increased to between 450 and 540 rounds.

Table 2   *Units of fire*
Location of Ammunition Stocks by Command Level

25X1

Type of Ammunition	Regiment or Division	Army	Air Army	Front	Total
Total	**6.25**	**1.35**	**0.75**	**8.80**	**18.15**
Small arms	1.0	0.15	0.75	1.0	3.90 [a]
Artillery	1.0	0.30		1.95	3.25
Tank	2.25	0.4		2.6	5.25
Antiaircraft	2.0	0.5		3.25	5.75

[a] The total 3.90 (instead of 2.90) is in the original Soviet document.

locations of the Soviet front- and army-level depots in East Germany

25X1

For divisions and regiments in East Germany, peacetime ammunition stocks include some in permanent bunkers and some on vehicles. In particular:

25X1

25X1

ammunition storage areas and to expand existing areas. By February 1980, nine storage depots were being expanded (figure 3) and seven new ones were under construction. Figures 3 and 4 illustrate this activity. When all construction is complete—possibly in early 1984—the front-level ammunition storage capacity in the GSFG will have more than doubled, from about 185,000 metric tons in 1976 to around 473,000 metric tons.[12] Blast walls have been constructed around all the ammunition storage buildings at these 16 depots.

At the army level, we have identified five ammunition storage depots. There was no significant increase in their capacity between 1976 and 1980. Blast walls were constructed around existing ammunition storage buildings, but any new shelters observed were replacements for older types and did not significantly change the storage capacities of the depots. We estimate that as of February 1980 the army-level depots in East Germany could store about 100,000 metric tons of ammunition. Table 6 in appendix C lists the precise

tanks in East Germany are loaded with ammunition during peacetime. If this is the case, the 5,000 Soviet tanks there could contain about 8,500 metric tons of ammunition.

25X1
25X1
25X1
25X1
25X1

25X1

Figure 2
Front and Army Conventional Ammunition Depots in East Germany

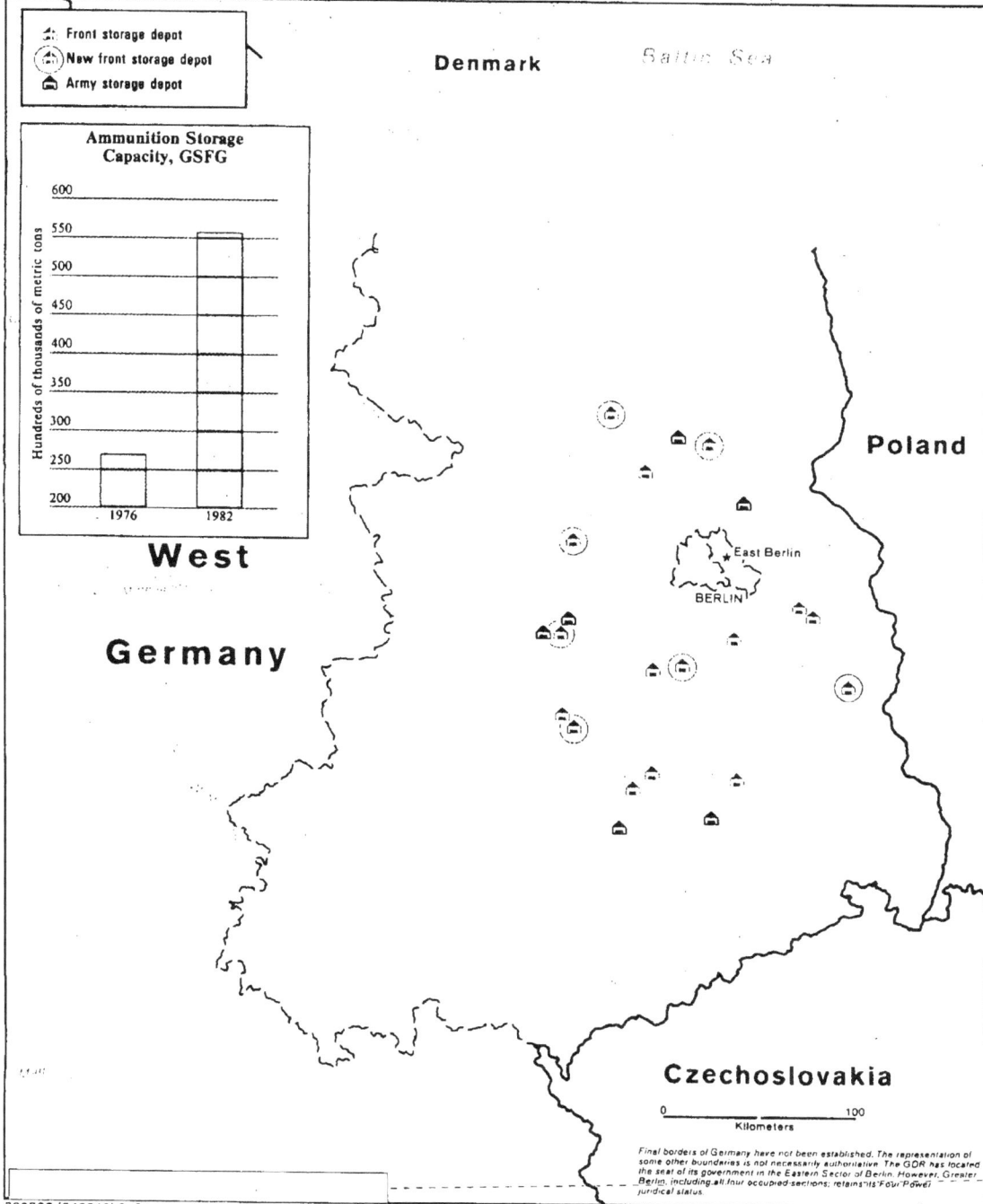

25X1

25X1

25X1

R70-14

25X1

25X1

11

25X1

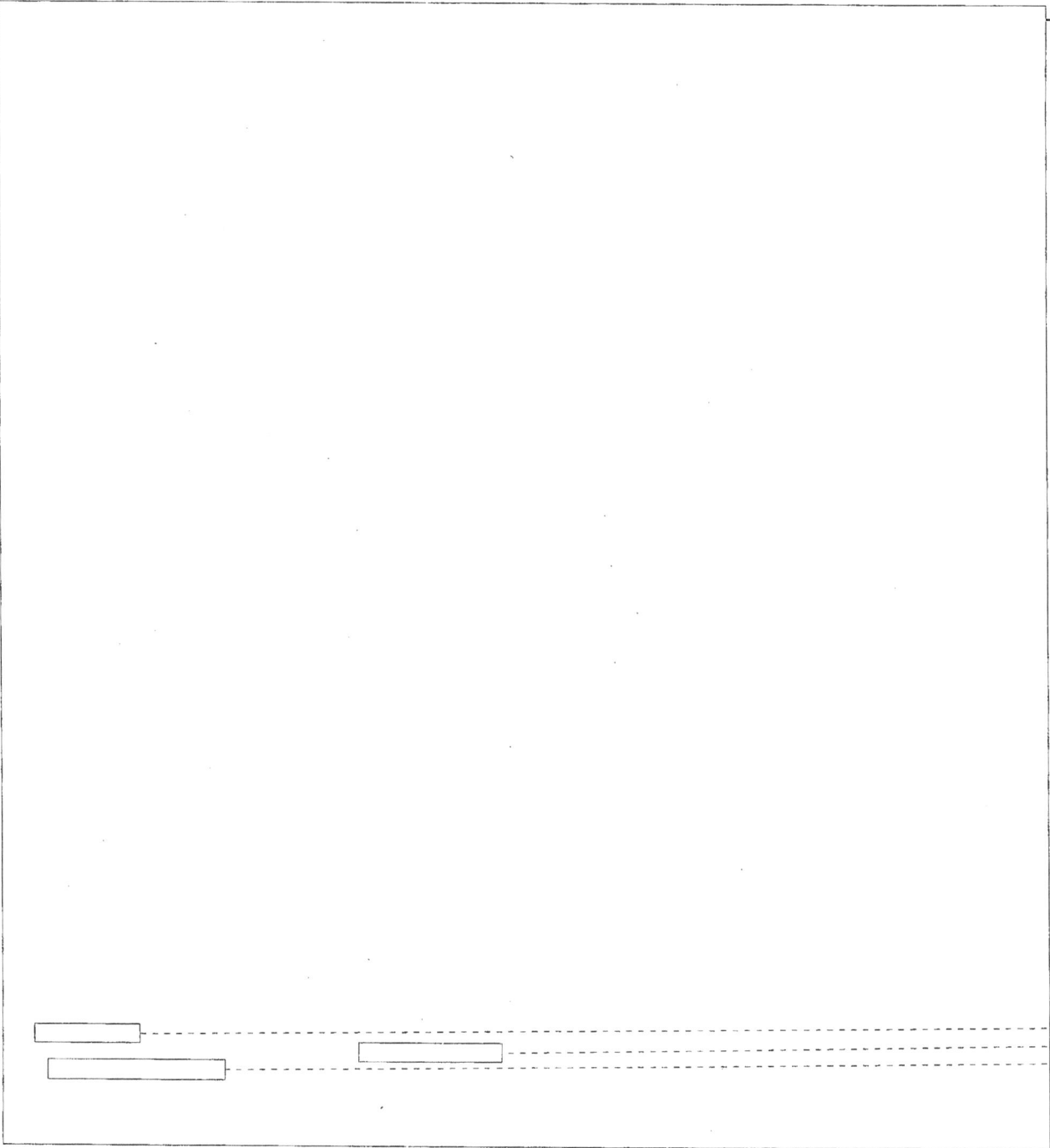

25X1

25X1

HR70-14

25X1
25X1
25X1

25X1

Body-19

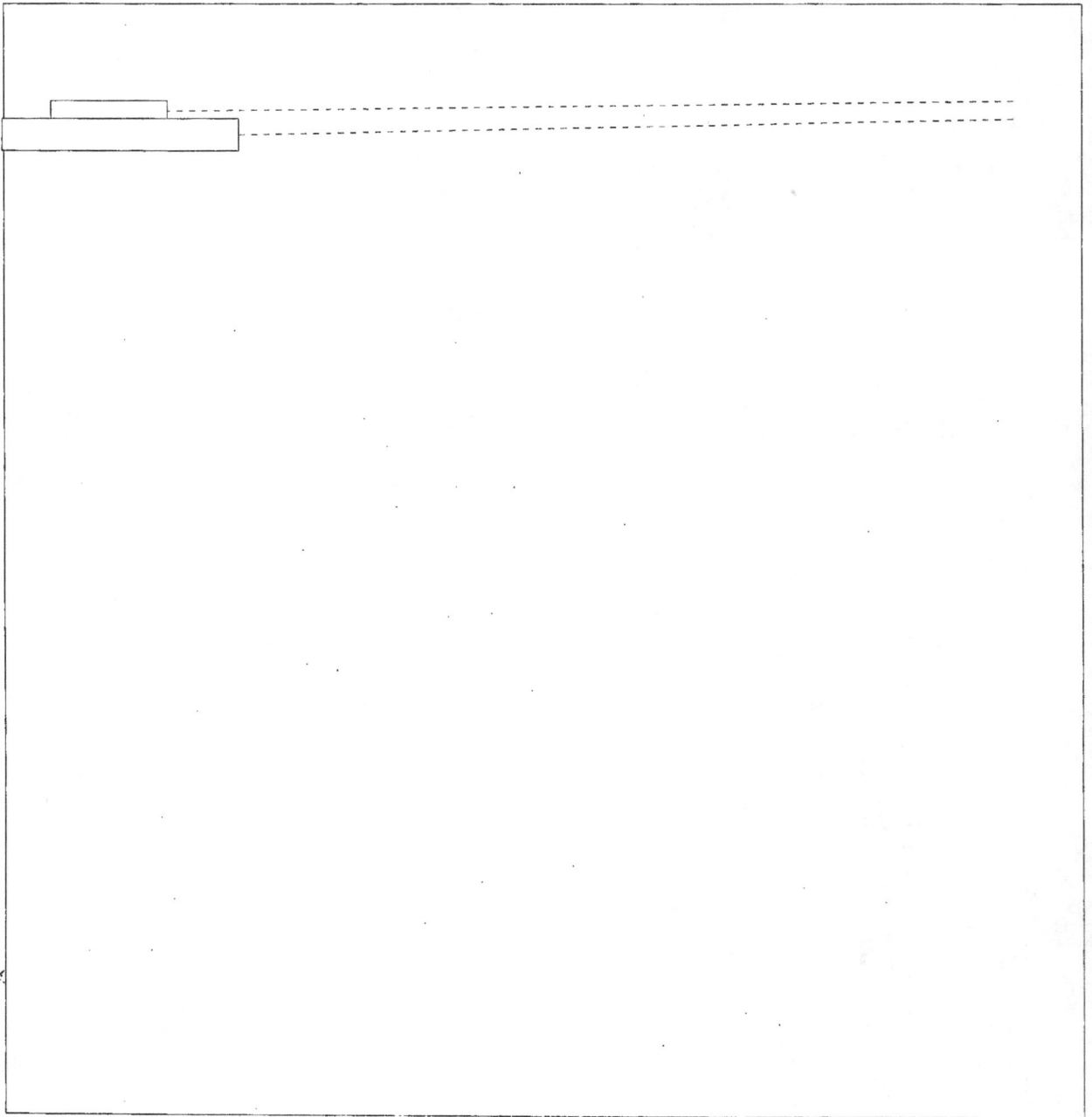

Body-20

25X1

We have no direct evidence that explains the expansion of ammunition depots in East Germany since 1976. There are at least two possible reasons for it, however:

- The Soviets may have revised their norms for conventional ammunition allocations in a modern war, as advocated by authors in the 1960s, and expanded their ammunition stockpiles in response to higher requirements.

- By the late 1970s, the Soviets may have begun to stockpile ammunition for TMO war reserves in conjunction with the formation in 1978 of the wartime CAF structure, thus providing a physical dimension to an organization that previously had only been planned.

We believe that during peacetime the Soviets probably supply current (training) operations from the ammunition stored on trucks in depots. Activity patterns noted [   ] during periods when units were exercising suggests that the trucks were used in the exercises—possibly to supply ammunition—and then returned to the ammunition depot parking area.

Warsaw Pact writings indicate that as divisions and armies move to a war status they are to transfer responsibility for their fixed facilities to the front command. This is because during combat the division and army commands are to be completely mobile, and their combat stocks will in effect be what they can carry in their trucks and combat vehicles. For short periods—during preparatory firing conducted at the outset of an operation, for example—the division and army artillery units could receive supplemental allocations, but these would have to be stored on the ground for almost immediate use. Ammunition is to be supplied during the course of an operation through the network of front and army supply bases.

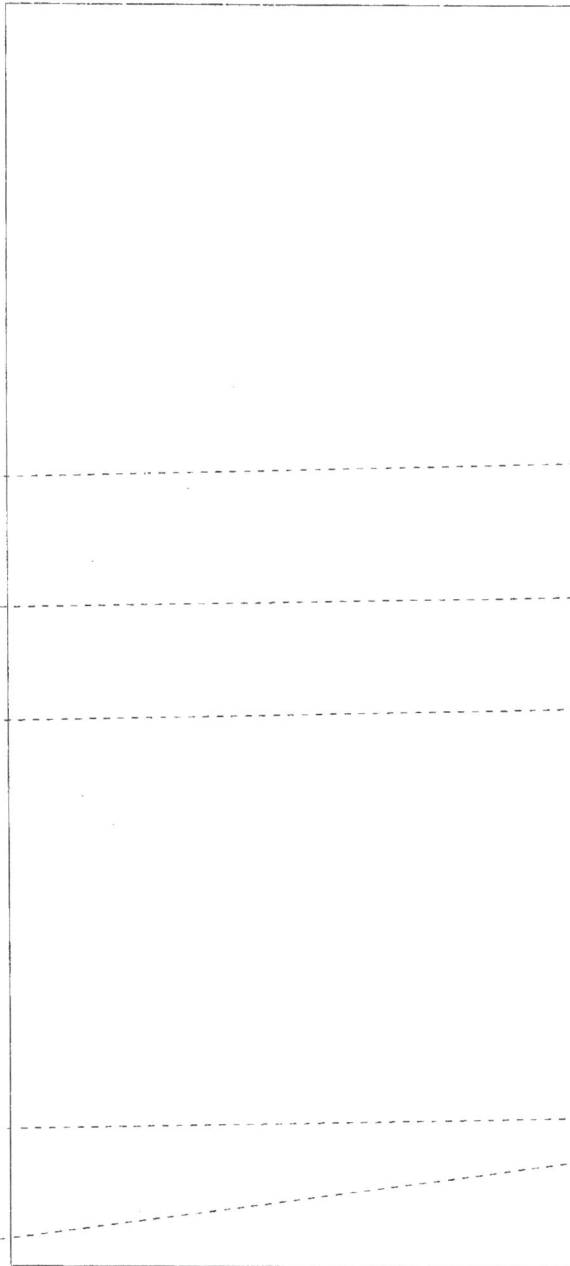

25X1

25X1

25X1

25X1

25X1
25X1

14

25X1

15.

25X1

Figure 6
Organization of a Soviet Mobile Rocket-Technical Base

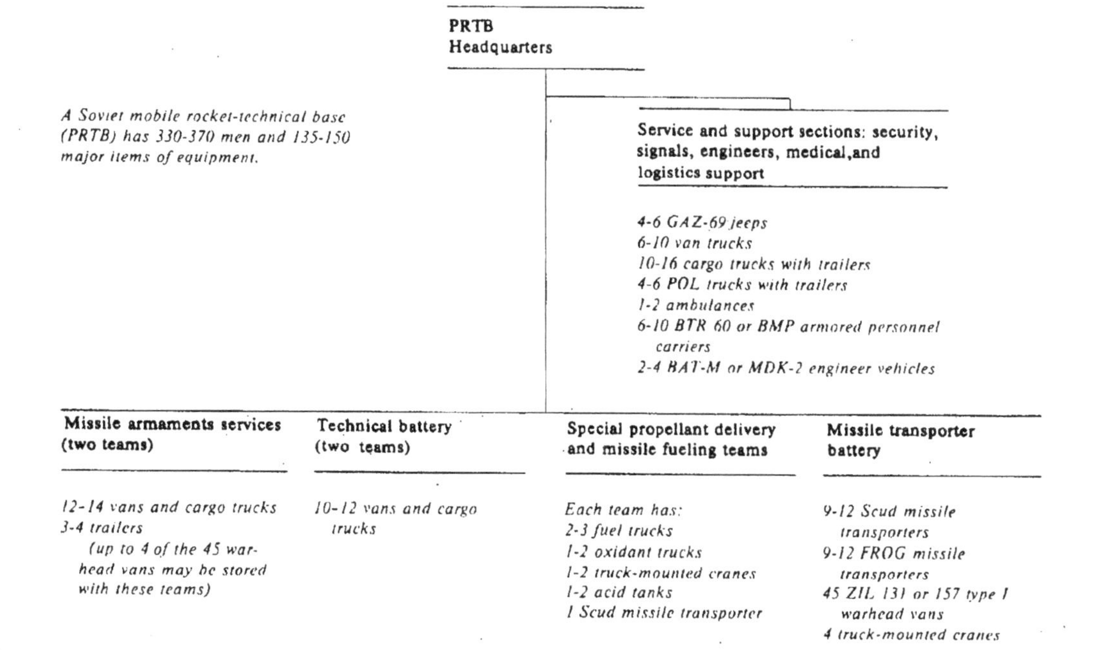

PRTB
Headquarters

A Soviet mobile rocket-technical base (PRTB) has 330-370 men and 135-150 major items of equipment.

Service and support sections: security, signals, engineers, medical, and logistics support

4-6 GAZ-69 jeeps
6-10 van trucks
10-16 cargo trucks with trailers
4-6 POL trucks with trailers
1-2 ambulances
6-10 BTR 60 or BMP armored personnel carriers
2-4 BAT-M or MDK-2 engineer vehicles

Missile armaments services (two teams)	Technical battery (two teams)	Special propellant delivery and missile fueling teams	Missile transporter battery
12-14 vans and cargo trucks 3-4 trailers (up to 4 of the 45 warhead vans may be stored with these teams)	*10-12 vans and cargo trucks*	*Each team has: 2-3 fuel trucks 1-2 oxidant trucks 1-2 truck-mounted cranes 1-2 acid tanks 1 Scud missile transporter*	*9-12 Scud missile transporters 9-12 FROG missile transporters 45 ZIL 131 or 157 type I warhead vans 4 truck-mounted cranes*

25X1

301392 1-84

25X1

we have identified 17 units of these three types in East Germany, as shown in figure 8 and table 7 (appendix C). These are:

- Eight PRTBs, which support seven entities—two front-subordinated Scud brigades and the rocket units of five armies. One PRTB is "extra," because in 1982 a third Scud brigade was disbanded and its equipment combined with the other two. The Soviets may adjust the configuration of their PRTBs to match the new missile brigade organization, or they

may keep the extra PRTB as it is (the number of missile launchers in East Germany has not changed).

- Seven ORPDs that provide additional nuclear weapons, to reinforce the PRTBs.

- Two Soviet custodial detachments, one at each Type VII nuclear warhead storage site.

25X1

25X1

16

25X1

Figure 7
Organization of a Soviet Independent Missile Transport Battalion

---

ORPD
Headquarters

A Soviet independent missile transport battalion (ORPD) has 200–250 men and 110–130 major items of equipment.

Service and support sections: security, signals, engineers, medical, and logistics support

2-3 GAZ-69 jeeps	6-10 BTR-60 or BMP armored
4-8 van trucks	personnel carriers
10-12 cargo trucks	2-4 BAT-M or MDK-2
4-6 POL trucks	engineer vehicles

Missile transport battery[a]

12 Scud transporters
12 FROG transporters
48 warhead vans
4-6 truck-mounted cranes

Surface-to-air missile technical battery[b]

18-24 MAZ or KAMAZ truck tractors with semitrailers
or
18-24 SA-4 or SA-6 SAM missile transporters

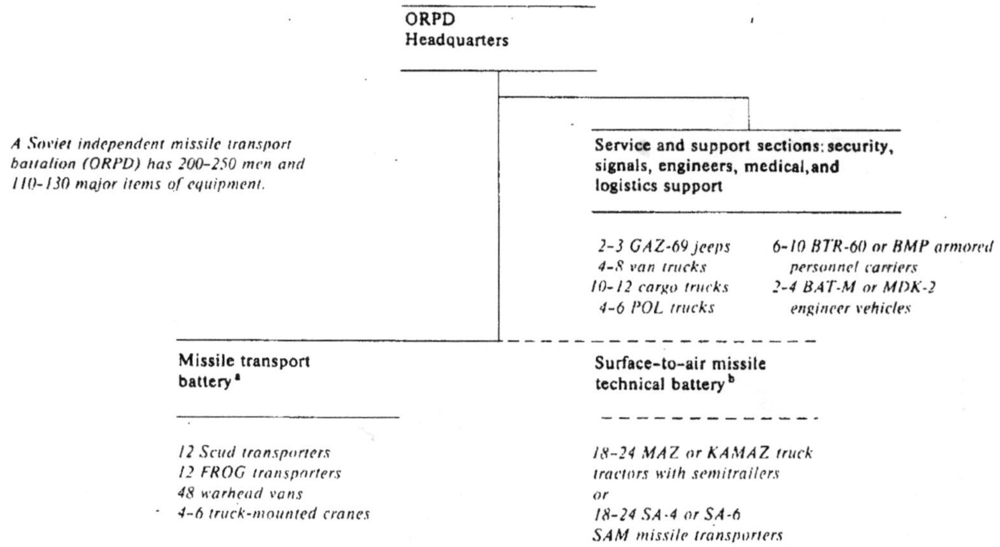

[a] The ORPD also has a missile armament services team for FROG or SS-21 missiles, which is probably associated with the missile transport battery.

[b] These batteries have been observed with ORPDs in the USSR since 1980. ORPDs in the groups of Soviet forces in other Warsaw Pact countries do not yet have this subunit.

25X1

301393 1-84

Nuclear Ammunition Requirements
Our information about Soviet perceptions of rocket and missile requirements comes from several sources:

25X1

- Soviet written doctrine of the mid-1970s indicates that a front might hold some 130 to 160 rockets and missiles.

- Several items written in the mid-1970s indicate that the Soviets anticipated using 300 to 400 nuclear missiles or rockets during a front operation. Other writings of that period indicate that about 160 to 180 would be used during the initial nuclear strike.

- One Soviet author indicated in the late 1960s that during a front operation each launcher would be allocated three rounds, two of which would be nuclear and one chemical.

25X1
25X1

17

25X1

Figure 8
Soviet Nuclear Weapon Support Units in East Germany

700798 (546840) 2-84

25X1

25X1

25X1

Pact writings, suggests that these personnel:

25X1
25X1
25X1

- Receive bulk POL products (transported via pipeline, rail, or waterway) and store them in large depots.

- Maintain the quality of these stocks, distribute them to military units, and maintain reserves.

- Maintain the depot facilities; this includes cleaning and periodically refurbishing storage tanks and maintaining the equipment used to handle POL products.

- Store and maintain the additional equipment that would be used by units mobilized for war to transport, store, and distribute POL during combat. This equipment would include tactical pipe sections and pipeline construction machinery, portable containers or reservoirs for field fuel depots, and equipment for tactical refueling points.

We conclude that the Soviets probably have amassed in East Germany a capability for nuclear warfare that is consistent at least with their planned requirements for a front.

25X1

- Repair the specialized POL-handling equipment.

25X1

Petroleum, Oil, and Lubricants

According to Soviet writings, the acquisition, handling, and distribution of petroleum, oil, and lubricants (POL) for Soviet ground forces is the responsibility of the Fuels Supply Service. Each echelon has a fuels supply officer who is in charge of POL-associated personnel and operations. He is subordinate to the deputy commander for rear services.

Fuels Supply Service personnel operate storage depots and fuel-handling units at all levels of the Warsaw Pact forces. Warsaw

ª Our estimate of the maximum number of warheads that can be transported is based on the number of warhead vans at PRTBs and ORPDs in East Germany.

POL Distribution in Peacetime

During peacetime, petroleum products are distributed throughout Eastern Europe through an extensive pipeline network (figure 9), as well as by road and rail. The "Friendship" pipelines consist of two dual conduits for petroleum: one originates in the Volga-Urals area of the USSR to carry crude oil to refineries at Plock (Poland) and at Schwedt and Luena (East Germany), and another runs from near Kuybyshev to serve Czechoslovakia and Hungary. A network of secondary pipelines distributes petroleum products within Eastern Europe.

25X1

25X1
25X1

at least 41 large bulk POL storage depots are located in the GSFG (figure 10). Each can store between 4,000 and 20,000 metric tons, for a combined capacity of nearly 500,000 metric tons. These depots probably provide the initial terminus and storage points for most of the fuel delivered to the GSFG.

25X1
25X1
25X1

25X1

25X1

25X1

Figure 9
Major POL Facilities in Eastern Europe

Denmark — Sweden — Baltic Sea

Röstock

Gdańsk

Hamburg

Szczecin

West

Schwedt

Germany

Berlin
E. Berlin

Płock

East

Poznań

Germany

Warsaw

Poland

Łódź

Leuna   Leipzig

Soviet
Union

Frankfurt

Most

Prague

L'vov

Czechoslovakia

Kalush

Brno

Munich

Košice

Mukachevo

Vienna

Bratislava

Miskolc

Austria

Budapest
Százhalombatta

Switz.

	Oilfield
	Refinery
	Pipeline
	Tanker port

Hungary

Romania

Szeged

0   200
Kilometers

Italy

Yugoslavia

Boundary representation is
not necessarily authoritative.

25X1

700799 (A03070) 2-84

25X1

25X1

Figure 10
Front and Army POL Depots in East Germany

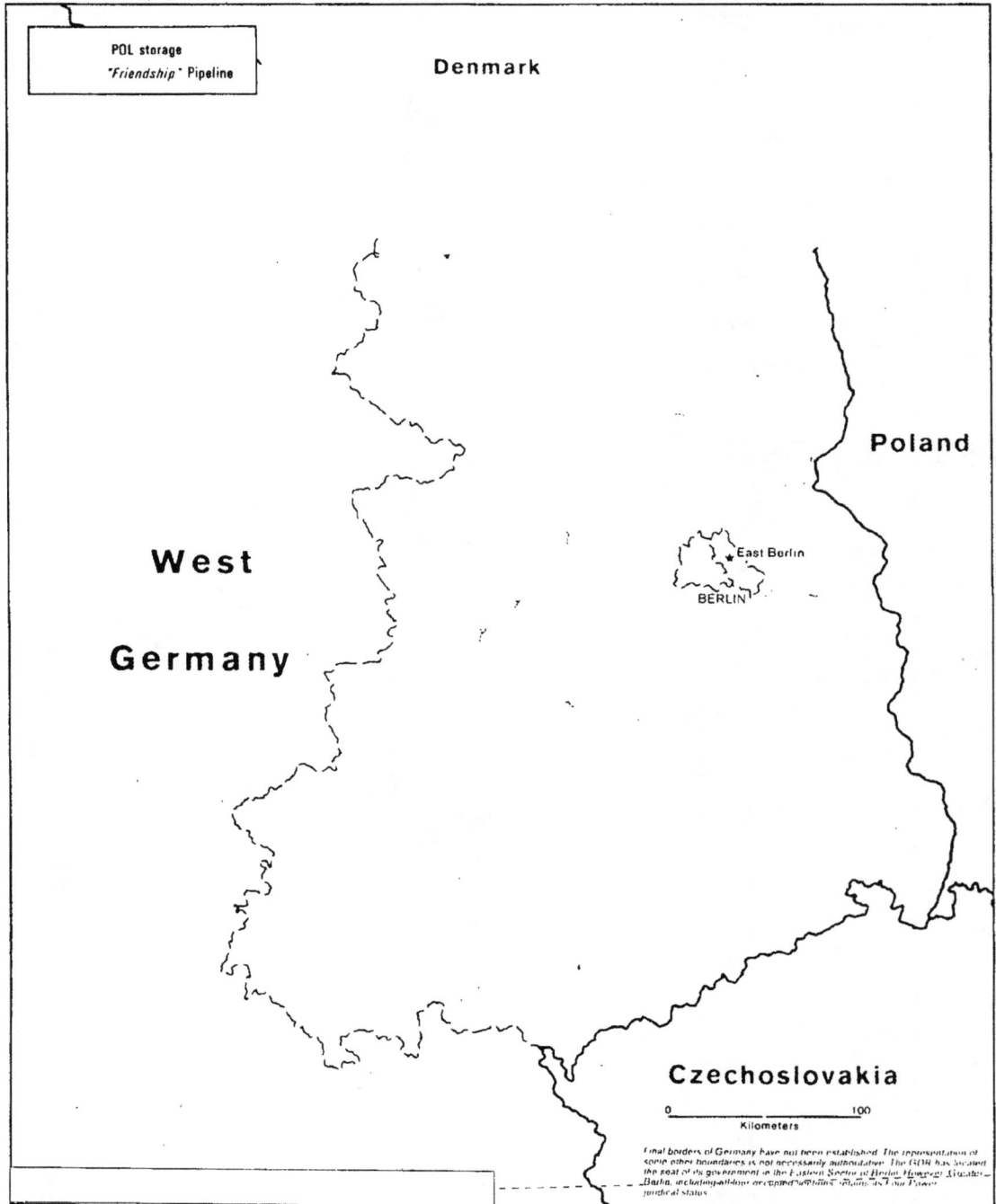

POL storage
"Friendship" Pipeline

Denmark

Poland

West

Germany

★ East Berlin
BERLIN

Czechoslovakia

0   100
Kilometers

Final borders of Germany have not been established. The representation of
some other boundaries is not necessarily authoritative. The GDR has located
the seat of its government in the Eastern Sector of Berlin. However, Greater
Berlin, including all four occupied zones, retains its Four Power
juridical status.

25X1

700800 (546840) 2-84

21

25X1

25X1

POL is unloaded from rail tank cars, stored at the depot, and then reloaded into tank trucks that come from Soviet units to the depot for resupply. These depots also store and distribute various types of packaged oils, fluids, and lubricants. Table 8 in appendix C lists the exact locations of these fixed POL depots.

and Soviet writings) that each of these depots has a fuel and lubricants unit (*chast' goryuchiy i smazochnyye materialy—GSM*). Figure 11 shows the POL depot at Finsterwalde, with its GSM, or POL unit. Each GSM probably consists of:

- A headquarters section (*shtab chast'*).
- A technical subunit (*tekhnicheskaya chast'*), responsible for receipt and resupply of POL.
- A unit POL laboratory (*laboratoriya chast'*), which tests POL products.
- A physical security platoon (*okhranyy vzvod*).
- A firefighting section (*pozharnaya komanda*).
- A medical section (*meditsinskiy punkt*).

Each GSM probably has 80 to 100 men, of whom about 30 are directly involved in the unloading and dispensing of POL and the maintenance of storage areas and tanks. The rest probably have administrative, support, or security duties.

In addition, each of these GSMs has 20 to 30 bays of vehicle storage, which probably contain a jeep or two, eight to 10 cargo trucks, a truck-mounted crane, and eight to 10 truck- or trailer-mounted POL pumping stations. Most of the 41 POL depots also have storage space for the equipment of a tactical-level field refueling point (PZP).

In addition to the 41 major GSFG depots, smaller POL storage facilities are located with all active combat and support units.

We have not estimated the capacity of these depots, but we judge that each can contain an amount at least equal to the POL lift capacity of its unit and possibly more. The experience of former servicemen suggests that in peacetime these depots hold the fuels needed for daily training and administrative support functions, as well as the reserve for initial combat requirements.

In the event of hostilities, the regiment or battalion would load POL from its depot as it prepared to leave its garrison. Warsaw Pact writings suggest that after the unit's departure the POL products remaining in the depot would be transferred to the administrative control of the front supply base.

POL Distribution in Wartime

Unclassified Soviet writings indicate that in wartime the fuel supply process within the area controlled by a front includes three general stages:

- Delivery by field pipeline (*polevoy magistral'nyy truboprovod*) from main pipelines or from railway and waterway depots to the front's rear area.
- Transportation by tank truck (*avtotsisterna*) from the field pipeline terminus to field fuel depots (*polevoy sklad goryuchego*) and troop fuel depots (*voyskovoy sklad goryuchego*).
- Delivery by POL trucks and trailers (*avtotoplivozapravshchiki*) from field and troop depots to units deployed for combat operations.

Delivery to the Front's Rear Area. According to their classified writings, the Soviets acknowledge that during a war it will be impossible to stockpile near the combat area the large quantities of fuel the troops will require during operations. The authors also know they cannot rely on rail and motor transport alone, but must integrate the use of all means of POL transport, including pipelines, to assure adequate fuel supplies to advancing troops.

We believe that in the initial period of a war the operating units are to be resupplied by motor transport from fixed POL depots. Soviet and East European authors indicate, however, that, in the course of a front's operation, pipelines are to be the main means of fuel delivery, and that these are to run from the refineries in the rear to the front forward supply bases and branches and to airfields. They realize that it would take time to extend the existing stationary pipelines with tactical ones, and that the extensions might not be fully effective until the 10th or 12th day of operations. As early as the mid-1960s, Pact planners were advocating the pre-positioning of pipeline

25X1
25X1
25X1
25X1
25X1
25X1
25X1
25X1
25X1
25X1
25X1
25X1
25X1
25X1

25X1

25X1

equipment in areas where its use would be most likely, so that the pipeline units (which could be brought to full strength in a few days) could begin laying pipe as soon as possible. When such tactical pipelines are fully operational, the Soviets expect them to provide about one-third of the fuel required during a front operation.

The Soviets have made extensive preparations for their rear-area fuel distribution system. For example, an East European author has indicated that in time of war the national pipelines would be used by the military. In the late 1970s, British tour officers

25X1

23

25X1

discovered a stepdown valve in East Germany with which tactical pipe could be coupled to the main pipeline. We conclude, therefore, that the main pipelines in Eastern Europe would be militarized during wartime.[18]

Equipment for tactical pipeline units and over 700 stacks of pipe—enough for some 1,200 to 2,200 km of pipeline—are dispersed among 12 of the 41 POL depots in central and southern East Germany (figures 12 and 13). Vehicle storage capacity and equipment observed indicates that over 800 items of equipment have been pre-positioned, to be used by pipeline construction battalions and by a number of tactical pipeline construction units, POL transport companies, and support and service units. At least one of the battalions is equipped with automatic pipelaying equipment. One Soviet author has indicated that the main purpose of these tactical pipeline units is to set up field pipelines progressively behind advancing troops.

Delivery to the Operational-Tactical Rear. Wartime movement of POL from a front's forward bases and branches to the rear areas of the various armies will involve the use of motor transport vehicles to carry it from pipeline terminals to field and troop fuel depots.

In the mid-1960s at least one Soviet author pointed out that the use of cargo trucks loaded with cans of fuel would not be adequate to supply POL in combat. He noted that only one-third to one-fourth of the military's existing lift capacity was made up of tanker trucks and that even in the civilian economy there was a shortage of trucks especially designed to carry POL.

In addition, instead of loading fuel

drums on the bed of a general purpose truck to deliver fuel, they now fit the truck with a single large tank, effectively converting it temporarily to a tanker.

25X1
25X1
25X1
25X1
25X1
25X1

25X1

We also have observed some equipment of this type at major POL depots in East Germany. We cannot determine precisely how much is pre-positioned in East Germany, however, because some items—portable fuel reservoirs, some types of pumping units, and technical equipment, for example—probably are stored in warehouses and cannot be identified using satellite imagery.

25X1

25X1

Delivery to the Tactical Rear. The goal of all this effort is to ensure that advancing troops have an uninterrupted fuel supply. Soviet authors note that the task is complicated by the complete mechanization of their forces, the emphasis on maneuverability in modern operations, and the rapidity of the planned advance. They stress the importance of effecting the final stage of delivery, so that the advancing tactical units will not be brought to a halt by a lack of fuel.

25X1

25X1

To accomplish this, the Soviets introduced field refueling points (*polevoy zapravochnyy punkt*, PZP) in the early 1970s. Analysis of satellite imagery and Soviet press articles indicates that each PZP consists of tank trucks and trailers equipped with mounted pumping devices and trucks for transporting portable reservoirs and fueling aisles. PZP units can refuel

25X1

25X1

25X1

[18] We suspect that main pipelines now probably are controlled by the TMO and not by the front. For one reason, the higher echelon TMO wartime structure did not exist when the articles attributing main pipelines to fronts were written. For another, these pipelines provide petroleum products to several Warsaw Pact countries, which implies that their controlling authority in wartime is to be responsible for allocating fuel throughout an area much greater than we would anticipate for a front's operations.

[19] See section on Motor Transport Units in East Germany.

25X1

25X1

25X1

Figure 12
Soviet Tactical Pipeline Equipment Pre-Positioned in East Germany

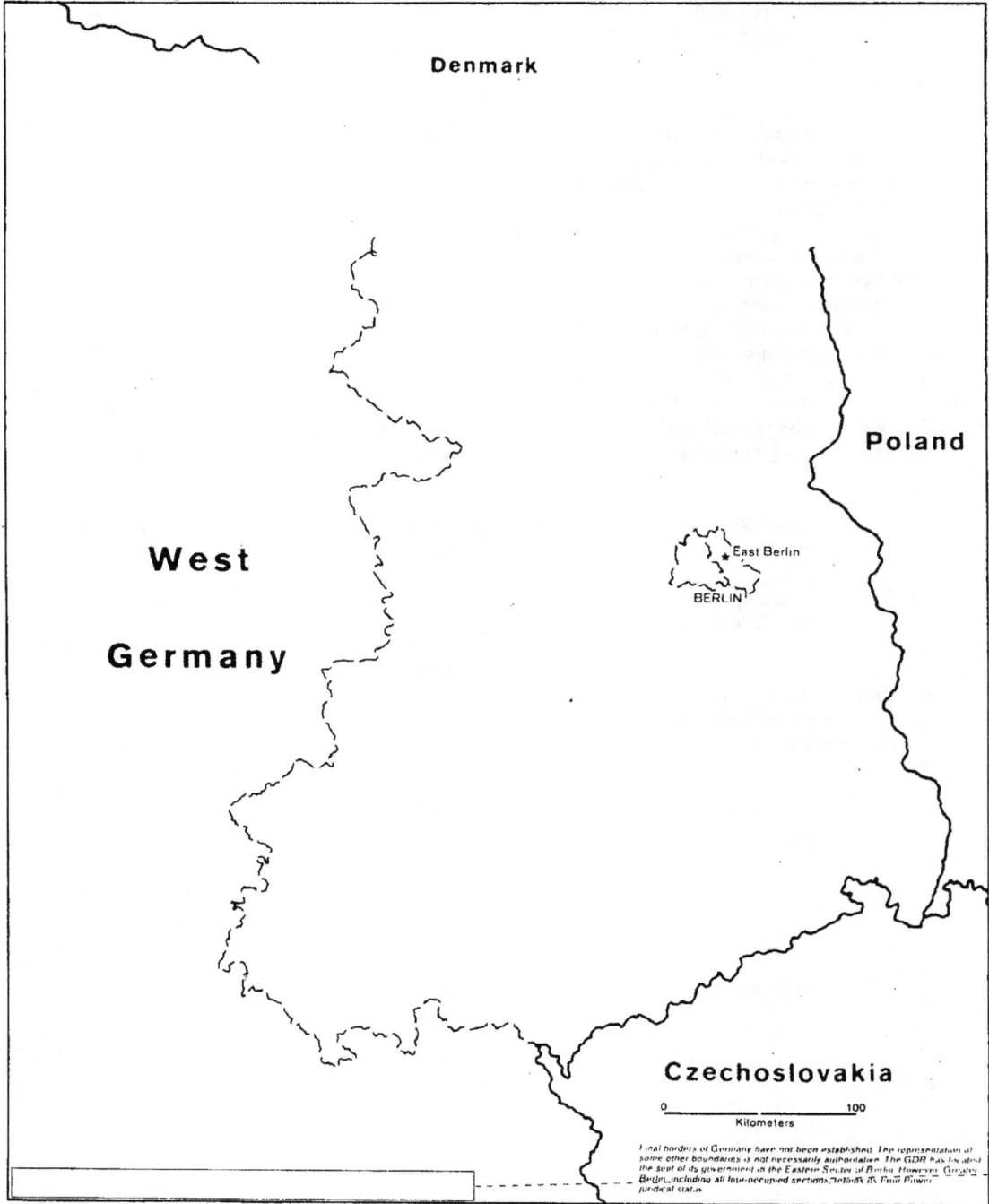

Denmark

Poland

West

Germany

★ East Berlin
BERLIN

Czechoslovakia

0   100
Kilometers

Final borders of Germany have not been established. The representation of some other boundaries is not necessarily authoritative. The GDR has located the seat of its government in the Eastern Sector of Berlin. However, Greater Berlin, including all four-occupied sectors, retains its Four Power juridical status.

700801 (546840) 2-84

25

25X1

25X1

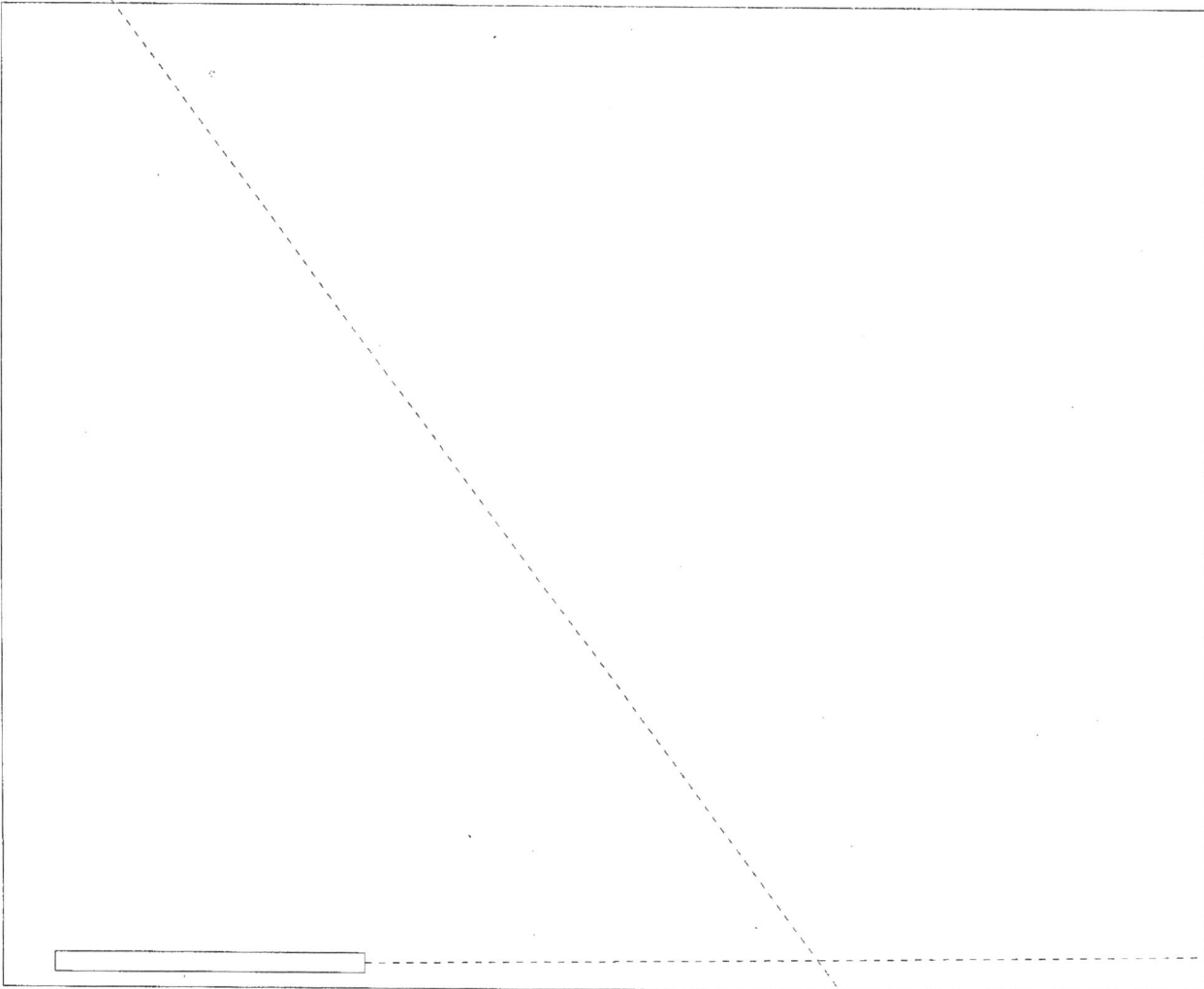

25X1

several vehicles simultaneously. The number of vehicles the PZP can refuel depends on the number and capacity of its pumping devices. Usually eight to 12 refueling stands (PZP-8, PZP-12) are installed for use with fuel tank trucks and 12 to 24 refueling stands (PZP-12, PZP-24) for use with fuel transfer pumps. Figure 15 shows a PZP unit in operation during a Soviet exercise in Mongolia.

is usually deployed in pairs to provide up to 48 fueling points. We believe the PZP-24 enables the Soviets to refuel an entire battalion in a matter of minutes. Equipment for mobile PZPs has been pre-positioned at POL depots in East Germany (figures 11 and 13).

25X1

25X1
25X1
25X1

The number of refueling stands and pumping devices deployed depends on the size of the units to be fueled. The PZP-24,

25X1 25X1

25X1

25X1

25X1

The Soviets also have fueling aisles, which resemble PZPs but are fixed, at each major POL depot in East Germany. These may be intended to provide rapid refueling of reserve or second-echelon forces advancing toward the battle zone.

25X1

POL Requirements
The Soviet military carefully plans its need for petroleum, quarterly and yearly.[20] Each Fuels Supply Service officer lists all the equipment in the unit he supports, the fuel and lubricant consumption rates for each type, and the rate at which the unit intends to operate its equipment. After the appropriate computations, he adjusts his total POL requirement upward to account for evaporation, waste, maintenance running, climate, and—presumably—pilferage. These projections are merged at successively higher headquarters

and ultimately are included in the five-year plan to become part of the goals for the civilian ministries that supply petroleum.

25X1

It is our judgment, based on Warsaw Pact writings about other classes of supply that petroleum stocks in peacetime probably include certain portions allocated for current training and others that are set aside as untouchable reserves (NZ). The NZ probably consists in peacetime of stocks sufficient for about three months of combat.

25X1
25X1
25X1

25X1

Sometime during the late 1960s the Soviets apparently increased their estimates of the amount of POL required for a front operation. In the mid-1960s one author estimated that 230,000 to 270,000 metric tons of all types of fuels would be required for an operation

25X1

25X1

25X1

25X1

25X1

to a depth of 2,000 km, and another noted that some 180,000 metric tons would be necessary for an operation 1,000 km deep. From a rough average of these figures, we conclude that during the mid-1960s the Soviets planned to consume about 150,000 metric tons in a front operation extending to a depth of about 1,000 km

By the late 1960s these figures had changed, and written Soviet doctrine was estimating that some 250,000 to 300,000 metric tons would be required for a 1,000-km operation—about twice the earlier estimate. Soviet writings suggest that this increase may

have been occasioned by the complete mechanization of Soviet ground forces, which was achieved in the early 1960s.

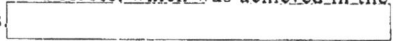

25X1

As has been noted above, however, the Soviets calculate the size of a front's peacetime stockpile not on the amount of fuel required for a specific front operation but on another concept—the amount the front would need for the first three months of a war and for training and administrative activities. Our analysis of Soviet writings and our knowledge of Soviet methods for estimating stockpile requirements suggest that requirements for a front's war reserve stocks could

25X1

25X1

amount to 830,000 or even 990,000 metric tons.[21] We cannot, however, estimate the amounts of fuel required for training or administrative uses.

25X1

25X1

POL, like other materials, is to be stored at various echelons in the military hierarchy. The requirements shown in table 3 (taken from Soviet writings) indicate that about 40 percent of all POL is to be stored at front depots, about 40 percent at army depots, and about 20 percent with troop units. (Of the POL stored at the army level, about two-thirds would be at ground army and one-third at air army depots.) If the estimated 830,000 to 990,000 metric tons that the front might stockpile in peacetime is distributed in this manner, 330,000 to 400,000 metric tons are in depots at the front and army levels and 160,000 to 200,000 metric tons in depots at the division level.

POL Stocks in East Germany

more than 600,000 metric tons of POL could be stored at Soviet installations throughout East Germany. Specifically:

- We believe the 41 major Soviet depots currently could contain up to about 475,000 metric tons of POL. Seven of the 41 were constructed after 1974, and all are now being expanded.

- Each of the 24 active Soviet airfields in East Germany has at least one aviation fuel depot, and some have two. Altogether, they could store some 60,000 to 90,000 metric tons of additional POL. These depots also have expanded since 1974. In addition, positions for collapsible fuel bladders have been constructed since 1968. These are apparently to permit the rapid expansion of aviation fuel depots, if necessary.

- We have not estimated the capacity of depots located at or near Soviet division and regiment installations, but we judge that each probably contains at least enough POL to load the vehicles in the unit. This could amount to around 3,500 to 4,000 metric tons of POL for each of the 19 Soviet divisions in East Germany, or a total of 65,000 to 75,000 metric tons.

25X1

[21] The method used to calculate this estimate is described in appendix B

25X1

Table 3 — *Refills*
Location of POL Stocks
by Command Level

25X1

25X1

	Regiment or Division	Army	Air Army	Front	Total [a]
Total	**4.1**	**1.16**	**14.05**	**14.9**	**27.80**
Gasoline	1.7	0.46	3.0	2.9	5.25 [a]
Diesel	2.4	0.7	3.55	4.5	7.65 [a]
Aviation			7.5	7.5	15.0

25X1

Warsaw Pact writings indicate that all of these fixed POL depots would become part of the front's supply base during wartime. The divisions and regiments, which are to be completely mobile, are to transfer their fixed facilities to front control as they prepare for deployment.

25X1

25X1

25X1

Force Reconstitution

The Soviets have given great attention to methods of maintaining the combat strength of their forces. They have developed a network of medical care facilities and organizations for treating the sick and wounded as far forward in the battle area as possible, and organizations for repairing damaged equipment as quickly as possible.

25X1

Medical Support

According to

DIA analysis, medical support for Soviet military forces is designed to care for sick and injured troops without taking them any farther from their units or keeping them any longer than is absolutely necessary. A system of triage provides for the screening of patients at lower command echelons and their evacuation to higher echelons (still in the forward area) for

25X1

25X1

25X1

25X1

specialized medical care.[22] The emphasis on evacuation reduces the need for a cumbersome medical structure within combat units, and the emphasis on providing medical care in the forward area minimizes the drain on manpower caused by battle casualties.

Military Medical Care in Peacetime

Soviet divisions provide little medical care during peacetime. Tactical units' tables of organization and equipment provide for medical personnel and equipment, the medical personnel—particularly at company and battalion level—do little more than inspect quarters and mess halls and teach personal hygiene and first aid. At the regimental level they provide some medications in a small dispensary or clinic, referring patients who require treatment to a military polyclinic (outpatient facility) in the area. Divisions have hospitals, or clinics, but these reportedly are small (50 to 100 beds) and provide only limited care.

in peacetime most medical care is provided for Soviet military personnel at higher echelons through a network of garrison and military district polyclinics and hospitals. Military units send patients first to the polyclinics, which have roughly the same medical specialties as the garrison hospitals. The polyclinics treat some of them on an outpatient basis and send the others to a hospital.

A garrison hospital is located in permanent buildings at every city where there is a military installation. It generally contains about 600 beds and can provide qualified, though limited, care through a number of specialized medical departments. Garrison hospitals reportedly may employ some 200 personnel; in peacetime many of these probably are civilians.[23]

---

[22] Triage (sorting) is the medical personnel's immediate assessment of casualties to identify those to evacuate to the next medical echelon immediately, those to treat prior to evacuation, those to treat and return to their combat units, and those for whom treatment is futile.

[23] Soviet authorities prefer to employ civilian doctors during peacetime—their wages are lower than military wages for corresponding skills. In addition, civilians do not move from place to place as frequently as military personnel and thus provide more stable hospital staffs.

Military district hospitals reportedly are larger than garrison hospitals and contain 800 to 2,000 beds. Some 500 to 750 military and civilian personnel provide a full range of medical services through some 18 to 22 specialized medical departments.[24] Patients probably are admitted by referral from a military district polyclinic, but the hospital undoubtedly accepts cases referred by garrison hospitals as well. The polyclinics at this echelon provide advanced outpatient care

25X1

25X1

25X1

Military Medical Care in Wartime
25X1
Soviet writings indicate that the system for providing medical care on the battlefield has been designed to maintain the combat strength of the forces by treating casualties as soon as possible and as far forward as possible in the combat zone or evacuating them promptly, and by combating the spread of disease and epidemics. Soviet authors anticipate that a modern battlefield will have no fixed fronts but will have sudden concentrations of seriously wounded, particularly as a result of nuclear attacks. Soviet military doctrine, which emphasizes mobility and flexibility in combat, also calls for a medical capability to respond quickly.

25X1

25X1

25X1

Lower Echelon Medical Points. Former servicemen indicate that divisions provide almost as little medical care in wartime as in peacetime. Medical personnel in the tactical echelon are to concentrate on sorting casualties according to the type of attention required and evacuating them to appropriate specialists quickly.

25X1

25X1

During combat, medical corpsmen and paramedics locate casualties and take them to the company or battalion casualty collection point. Their primary concern is to apply first aid and evacuate the casualties to regimental collection points.

25X1

At the regimental medical point (*polkovoy meditsinskiy punkt*, PMP) casualties are examined for the first time by a physician. The PMP provides only the most

25X1 •

25X1

[24] the chiefs of these departments also serve as staff officers on the military district medical staff.

25X1

25X1

25X1

30

25X1

basic forms of treatment, however; its primary function is to organize the evacuation of casualties to the division's medical point.

The division's medical point (*divizionnoy meditsinskiy punkt*) is maintained by its medical battalion (*mediko-sanitarnyy batal'yon*, MSB—*medsanbat*). It is intended to handle about 400 patients during a day of active combat. The medsanbat's primary purpose is the diagnosis of wounds so that casualties may be evacuated to appropriate field hospitals. It has enough vehicles to evacuate 80 men in one lift.

The division medical point can treat patients who might be expected to recuperate in a week or two, and it can perform minor or emergency surgery. Limitations of personnel and facilities require postponement of most surgical operations, however, until casualties arrive at a field hospital.

Army-Level Medical Detachments. According to Soviet writings, most battlefield medical care is provided by the independent medical detachment (*otdel'niy meditsinskiy otryad*, OMO). We believe these detachments are subordinate to the front commander, at least administratively, but are assigned or attached to individual armies to provide medical support where it is most needed. The front maintains reserves of medical units, to be sent to armies that have more casualties than anticipated or to areas with mass casualties.

Former servicemen indicate that the OMO was developed during the mid-1970s, apparently to increase the flexibility and responsiveness of the Soviet medical establishment in combat. According to Soviet writings, an OMO is almost identical to the divisional MSB (it can do simple surgery) but can evacuate 160 casualties in a single lift. It is designed to deploy to the area where the casualties are and to do triage: a team of five to 10 surgeons diagnoses wounds, performs emergency surgery, and determines the field hospitals for each patient.

Because the OMO is subordinate to the front's medical authorities, it can serve as a medical reconnaissance unit, informing field hospitals of incoming patient loads and front medical officers of areas where the medical reserve might be required.

Front-Level Field Hospitals. Soviet writings indicate that an injured soldier receives his first specialized medical care at a front mobile hospital base (*frontovaya podvizhnaya gospital'naya baza*, FPGB). A front could be assigned six to eight FPGBs, depending on the operational plan. Each FPGB can contain as many as 25 hospitals of the seven basic types, plus ambulance and other units. A front would tailor each mobile hospital base to suit a specific situation, but in general each would contain some 6,500 beds and include:

- Field evacuation hospitals (*polevoy evakuatsionnyy gospital'*—300 beds), which provide initial observation of patients not previously diagnosed and evacuation to other field hospitals.

- Multiple-profile hospitals (300 beds), which provide treatment for more than one type of injury. For example, if many casualties experience bullet wounds as well as infectious diseases, the mobile hospital base might form a special hospital to treat the two problems simultaneously.

- Surgical hospitals (*khirurgicheskiy gospital'*—200 to 300 beds), which perform a wide range of surgical operations.

- Therapeutic hospitals (*terapevticheskiy gospital'*—200 to 300 beds), which are staffed and equipped to treat patients not requiring surgery.

- Neuropsychiatric hospitals (200 to 300 beds), which treat personnel for shock or other mental disorders.

- Infectious disease hospitals (*polevoy infektsionnyy gospital'*—200 beds). Most of these treat patients with simple contagious diseases such as grippe, enteric fever, or meningitis. A variant, the hospital for highly contagious diseases (100 beds), is protected by barbed wire and armed guards and provides treatment for such diseases as cholera, plague, smallpox, typhus, and yellow fever.

25X1

31

25X1

- Hospitals for the lightly wounded (*gospital' legkikh ranennykh*—1,000 beds), which provide treatment for patients requiring only about two hours of treatment or observation per day and who can be discharged in about a month.

- Specialized medical detachments, which probably consist of groups of specialists (in at least five fields) who are on call to assist mobile field hospitals.

- An independent medical transportation battalion (*otdel'nyy avtosanitarnyy batal'yon*), which evacuates casualties and moves the field hospital equipment to areas designated by front medical authorities.

- Other small detachments, such as blood banks, X-ray detachments, oxygen stations, and postal detachments.[25]

The front assigns one of its FPGBs to support each first-echelon army, according to Soviet writings. It holds additional FPGBs in the rear, so they can be deployed to areas with massive casualties or to support advancing armies. In action, the FPGB usually is deployed initially about 50 km behind the forward line of troops, near a major road and housed in tents (or in buildings such as schools). When the division's MSBs or the army's OMOs have advanced 120 to 150 km beyond this FPGB, the front sends another FPGB, which is established about 50 km behind the new forward line. Thus, the time required to evacuate a casualty to a front mobile hospital base is held to five or six hours.

Soviet authors indicate that neither the FPGB as a whole nor any one of its subordinate hospitals has enough vehicles to relocate independently. To move the entire FPGB, additional transport must be provided, presumably by a battalion subordinate to one of the front's motor transport brigades. The FPGB alone can probably handle the relocation of one of its subunits; the presence of a hospital transport company in the FPGB's independent medical transportation battalion implies that when one of the subordinate hospitals is to be relocated, trucks are sent from this

company. Presumably they return to the battalion when the move is complete and prepare to move another hospital.

25X1

The front rear hospital base (*frontovaya tylovaya gospital'naya baza*, FTGB) is the rearmost echelon in the Soviet operational-level medical establishment. According to Soviet writings, each front might have two or three FTGBs, each of which could have around 45 subordinate hospitals—or a total capacity of some 20,000 patients for the FTGB. These hospitals have the same specialties as those found in the mobile hospital bases but are usually located far to the rear, in permanent hospital facilities. (The permanent hospitals in East Germany are discussed below.) The mobile FPGB and its 25 hospitals are usually situated in one area, but the larger FTGB is usually spread over two or three locations.

25X1
25X1

An FTGB stays in the same place throughout the course of a front operation to care for patients who require moderate periods of hospitalization.[26] It might move at the conclusion of the operation, probably via railroad (relocation of a rear hospital base would require 700 to 800 trucks). Alternatively, one FTGB might be replaced after a front operation by another FTGB arriving by rail from the interior of the USSR.

25X1

Estimating Casualties. The Soviets expect this network of medical treatment facilities to be severely taxed, especially in the early days of a war. Medical staff officers at each command echelon estimate casualties as part of the operations planning process. We do not know exactly how they construct their estimates. In the mid-1970s, however, Soviet authors anticipated that in the course of a 15-day operation a front would require some 120,000 to 130,000 hospital beds, of which 40,000 to 50,000 would have to be available when operations commenced.

25X1

25X1

patients can remain in FTGB hospitals for up to two months.

25X1
25X1

---

[25] The general composition of an FPGB has been outlined in Soviet writings. Our estimates of its components' bed capacities, however, were derived from information provided by former Soviet servicemen. (TS NF NC OC)

32

25X1

25X1

25X1

medical goals—to treat casualties within a theater of operations without having to evacuate them to the USSR.

25X1

To care for such large numbers of casualties, the medical establishment has been designed to expand after the initial period of combat. The Soviets plan to care for the initial patient load in permanent hospital facilities in the early days of a war, and to deploy increasing numbers of mobile field hospital units as their armies advance.

25X1

Soviet Medical Facilities in East Germany
Quantity

(appendix C). We believe these are at least garrison-level hospitals, and some may be subordinate to the GSFG (that is, equivalent to the military district level). This is because they are large, independent facilities outside unit garrison areas, such as the one at Oranienburg illustrated in figure 17. (Division hospitals or clinics are likely to be small buildings in division garrison areas, and a regimental clinic is probably little more than a room in a barracks.) We cannot determine the echelon of individual hospitals, however, because we cannot estimate their bed capacity or the size of their staffs.

25X1

In peacetime these permanent hospitals provide specialized medical care to Soviet personnel stationed in East Germany. They are also the peacetime custodians of the mobile units' medical equipment, which is stored in buildings and sheds on their grounds. Such an equipment set is visible in figure 17.

25X1

In addition, the permanent Soviet hospitals in East Germany probably have several wartime missions. In the initial period of a war, according to Soviet writings [   ] they are to about double their patient capacity so as to accept casualties from advancing first-echelon armies. As the field hospital system becomes established, the buildings and grounds of some of the permanent hospitals probably will provide the physical location for the FTGB, the rearmost of the operational-level hospitals. This will enable the Soviets to achieve one of their primary

Undoubtedly the permanent hospitals where the mobile equipment is stored also will serve as mobilization sites for field medical units. This is a relatively recent development. During the 1960s, when their writings were emphasizing the use of nuclear weapons on the battlefield, the Soviets greatly increased the mobility of their combat forces. They soon realized, however, that the rear services were being left behind. They probably began pre-positioning mobile medical equipment at hospitals in East Germany sometime in the 1960s

25X1

25X1

25X1
25X1

By 1972 mobile medical equipment was stored at some 27 hospitals, and by 1982 it was stored at about three-fourths of the hospitals in East Germany (see table 9).

25X1

25X1

We cannot 25X1 determine, however, exactly what type of medical unit will be associated with a particular set. This is because:

- Although the types of hospitals are many and varied, the equipment sets appear to be nearly identical in configuration. The mobile equipment kit on the grounds of the Oranienburg hospital (figure 17) is an example.

25X1

- Study of equipment sets does not indicate the size of the hospitals that will use them. Some large hospitals are likely to be billeted in tents, which probably are stored in peacetime in warehouses (out of sight of imagery). Alternatively, the Soviets might plan to establish the larger field hospitals in existing facilities, such as hospitals or schools.

25X1

25X1

25X1

- In many cases it is not the equipment but the personnel associated with a hospital that determines its specialty. Therapeutic hospitals differ from infectious disease hospitals more in their patients and medical personnel than in their equipment.

25X1

25X1

33

25X1

Figure 16
Soviet Military Hospitals in East Germany

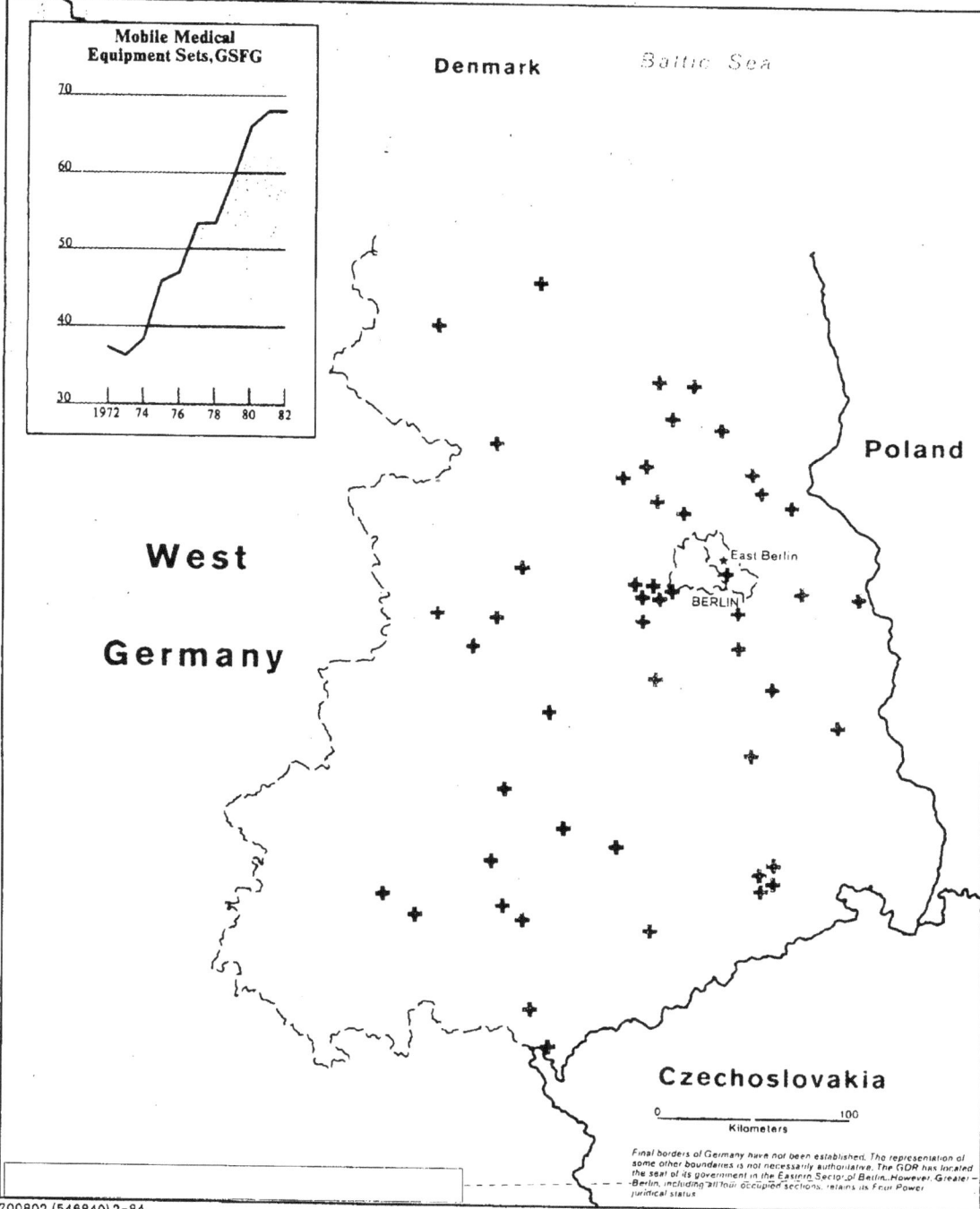

Mobile Medical
Equipment Sets, GSFG

Denmark

Baltic Sea

Poland

West

Germany

East Berlin

BERLIN

Czechoslovakia

0   100
Kilometers

Final borders of Germany have not been established. The representation of some other boundaries is not necessarily authoritative. The GDR has located the seat of its government in the Eastern Sector of Berlin. However, Greater Berlin, including all four occupied sections, retains its Four Power juridical status

25X1

700802 (546840) 2-84

34

25X1

25X1

25X1

This suggests that the Soviets have
committed themselves to developing their field medical capabilities in East Germany. We see no sign that
this commitment is likely to diminish soon. On the
contrary, we expect the Soviets to continue to expand
their mobile medical base—especially if, as we judge,
their casualty projections are increasing.

25X1

25X1

25X1 25X1

25X1

25X1

Although we do not know the true capacity of the hospital network in East Germany (permanent buildings plus stored mobile equipment), we judge that it is more than sufficient to satisfy the needs of a single front. Our knowledge of the system suggests some general estimates of the minimum and maximum capacity of permanent hospitals. If all the fixed hospitals in East Germany were garrison hospitals, they might accommodate 25,000 to 30,000 patients in peacetime, for example; and, if they were all GSFG-level hospitals, they might accommodate 40,000 to 100,000. In time of war these same hospitals probably would accept twice their normal patient load, to provide an initial capacity of some 60,000 to 200,000 casualties. This would be sufficient for as many as five fronts in the initial period of a war.

In addition, if the 65 identified mobile medical equipment sets are indications of 65 mobile field hospitals, then an additional 20,000 to 50,000 patients could be treated. (The Soviets may have other sets that we have not detected because of the way their equipment is stored in peacetime.) Finally, Soviet writings specify that civilian hospitals—and probably their staffs—are to be mobilized for military use during a war, and some garrisons vacated by divisions in first-echelon armies are to be converted to hospitals.

As these calculations make clear, the total capacity of the Soviet military medical establishment when it is expanded for extended combat operations is impossible to estimate. It almost certainly is extremely large.

Quality. The Soviets' apparent capability to provide medical facilities may be offset by inefficiencies within the medical system. the Soviets do not include a serviceman's blood type in his medical records. If this is the case, treatment of sick and wounded personnel would have to be delayed until their blood types could be determined.

Technical Support

Just as the Soviets' medical support is designed to treat casualties as far forward in the battle area as possible, their system for technical support is intended to repair damaged equipment and return it to combat units as quickly as possible. According to a British author who specializes in the study of the Soviet military press, the Soviets believe the only reliable sources of replacement equipment will be operational reserves and equipment that has been repaired in the battle zone. Their study of World War II experience has convinced them that new or rebuilt equipment will not reach their formations except during long marches, periods of preparation, or pauses between phases of an operation. The Soviets note, for example, that during the L'vov-Sandomir operation each tank and self-propelled gun was knocked out, on the average, two or three times.

25X1

25X1

25X1

25X1

Technical Support in Peacetime

According to Soviet writings equipment is inspected and serviced regularly during peacetime to ensure its reliability. In addition, the Soviets have designed safeguards into their equipment to protect against component failure and, if a failure occurs, to facilitate its repair. The scheduling of preventive maintenance, servicing, and periodic inspections is based generally on accrued kilometers or engine hours. The goal apparently is to maintain each unit's vehicles so that they may be

25X1

25X1

25X1

25X1

25X1

25X1

25X1

25X1

25X1

driven the maximum number of kilometers before their next scheduled maintenance.   25X1

According to Soviet writings   Soviet maintenance inspections are divided into three categories:

- Routine or daily inspections *(yzhednevnoye teknicheskoye obsluzhivaniye)*, which consist of checks by the operators to ensure that the vehicles are in good running order.

- Technical servicing No. 1 *(technicheskoye obsluzhivaniye* No. 1, or TO-1)*, which consists of a thorough check and servicing of the vehicle and its fluids, lubricants, suspension, drive train, and other subsystems.

- Technical servicing No. 2 *(technicheskoye obsluzhivaniye* No. 2, or TO-2)*, which is similar to TO-1 but includes more systems and subsystems, as well as such components as belts, spark plugs, ignition points, oil filters, and gaskets.

Soviet writings indicate that repairs also are divided into three categories:

- Running or light repair *(tekushchiy remont)*, which involves the immediate correction of minor problems occurring in normal use. It includes adjusting or replacing parts (such as carburetors and fuel pumps), making technical adjustments, and doing light welding or simple mechanical work.

- Medium repair *(sredniy remont)*, which consists of the replacement or overhaul of such major assemblies as engines, transmissions, or differentials. This may be needed to repair damage or may be scheduled at intervals based on kilometers accrued or engine operating hours. At the scheduled maintenance times, the engines, transmissions, and other components are replaced and the vehicles thoroughly inspected.

- Major or capital repair *(kapitalnyy remont)*, which consists of the complete rebuilding of the vehicle. All assemblies are either replaced or completely overhauled. Capital repair also is scheduled on the basis of accrued kilometers or operating hours.

During peacetime the Soviets use few of their vehicles regularly. Activity patterns noted through study of satellite imagery indicate that only about 10 to 15 percent of any unit's vehicles are used daily. The others are driven only rarely, and for most of the year are stored in conservation. Soviet writings and former servicemen indicate, however, that all are subjected to the Soviets' preventive maintenance regimen: 25X1 25X1 25X1

- The routine inspection is made before a vehicle is operated. For equipment in conservation, this inspection probably is made periodically—perhaps weekly.

- TO-1 is performed after each odd-numbered 1,000-km interval.

- TO-2 is performed after each even-numbered 1,000-km interval. For vehicles in conservation, it is performed every two years.

- An expanded version of TO-2 is performed on all vehicles after field training exercises.   indicate that a unit may spend seven to 10 days preparing its vehicles for return to storage. During this time all possible adjustments are made that do not require the removal of major assemblies such as engines or transmissions. In addition, worn parts are replaced, hydraulic and electrical systems are checked thoroughly and defective parts replaced, gaskets and fittings are checked and replaced as necessary, and the vehicle is spot painted.   25X1 25X1 25X1

- Medium and capital repairs are scheduled periodically. For vehicles that are operated regularly, these are based on the number of kilometers a vehicle has been driven. A T-55 tank, for example, is scheduled for medium repair at 6,000 km and for capital repair at 11,000 km after its introduction to an operational unit or after its last capital repair. Vehicles in conservation storage undergo capital repair every five years, unless a capital repair has been performed earlier on the basis of use   25X1 25X1

25X1

25X1

25X1 25X1

indicate that in tactical units (division and regiment level) the technical support capabilities are limited.

- Vehicle crews perform routine (daily) inspections and running (light) repairs. Technical officers in companies, battalions, and regiments inspect all vehicles periodically to make sure that maintenance is being performed properly.

- Battalion maintenance and repair teams *(remont-nyye gruppy,* RemG) supervise the vehicle crews in routine inspections and running repairs. These teams have a few mobile shop vans and a small garrison shop facility.

- Regimental maintenance companies perform emergency field repairs and minor repairs, in addition to routine maintenance. Some of these companies are divided into platoons with specific responsibilities. In a motorized rifle or tank regiment, for example, the maintenance company can include a tank repair platoon, a wheeled-vehicle repair platoon, an ordnance repair platoon, and an electrical repair platoon.

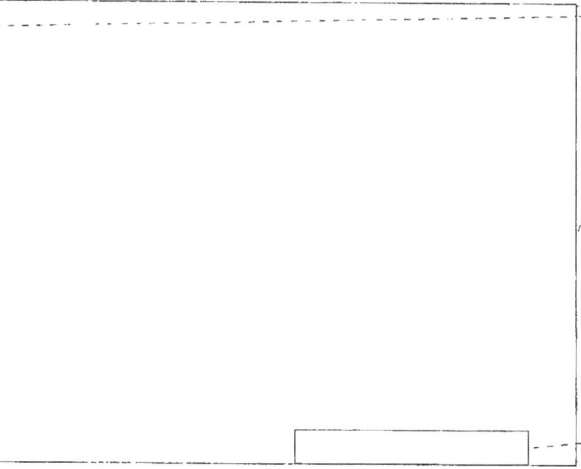

- Divisional maintenance battalions are the first units capable of performing more than routine inspections or running repairs. Each has some 200 personnel, usually divided into subunits that repair armored vehicles, wheeled vehicles, and ordnance. Most of the division maintenance battalion's work consists of routine inspections and running repairs, but it does some medium repairs—partly to train its mechanics, and also to maintain division vehicles. The battalion usually has 60 to 70 vehicles of its own and a garrison repair shop equipped with high bays and overhead cranes.

most medium and all capital repairs of Soviet equipment in East Germany are performed at Soviet nondivisional (that is, army- and front-level) maintenance facilities. Some of these handle tanks and armored fighting vehicles; others specialize in wheeled vehicles and engineer, artillery, signals, or missile support equipment; and still others rebuild engines. The locations of the Soviets' major fixed repair installations in East Germany are shown in figure 18.

25X1

Technical Support in Wartime

According to their writings, the Soviets plan to repair damaged equipment in wartime by concentrating repair units where damaged equipment is located. They plan to undertake first those repairs that can be completed quickly and to refer more extensive work to repair units of a higher command:

- *Tactical Units.* Regiments and divisions are to remove the equipment from the battlefield to damaged vehicle collection points *(sborniy punkt pov-rezhdennikh mashin, SPPM)* established along lines of communication. Running repairs and a few medium repairs will be made on the spot, using divisional resources. The Soviets believe that these tactical units should be able to perform all the running repairs and about 25 percent of the medium repairs needed during an operation.

- *Nondivisional Units.* Mobile maintenance units subordinate to fronts or attached to armies are to follow the tactical units and set up shop at the damaged vehicle collection sites. There they will perform all remaining medium repairs. If a vehicle requires repairs that cannot be made quickly, the mobile unit is to evacuate it to an army or front SPPM. In addition to medium repairs, front maintenance units are to perform as many capital repairs as they can. Most capital repairs, however, will be made in the rear area at fixed installations, which are subordinate either to the front or to the theater command.

25X1
25X1

25X1

25X1
25X1
25X1

ª See motor transport section.

38

25X1

Figure 18
Soviet Nondivisional Maintenance Facilities in East Germany

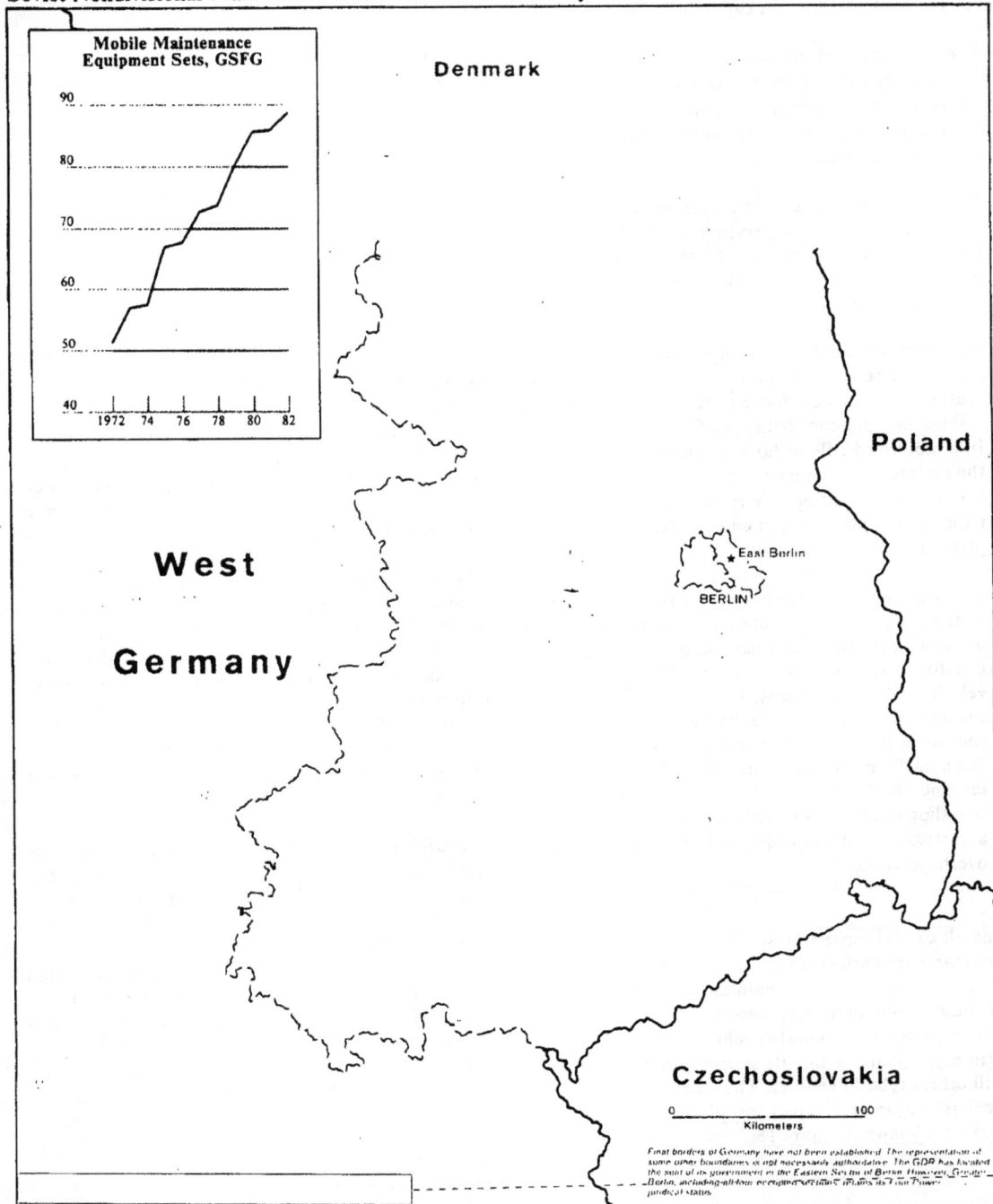

25X1

700803 (546840) 2-84

25X1

25X1

25X1

25X1

25X1

Soviet authors indicate that a front might have several types of units for the various repair tasks. These include:

- About two tank recovery battalions.
- One or two motor vehicle recovery battalions.
- Nine to 12 tank repair battalions.
- Thirteen to 15 motor vehicle repair battalions.
- Three or four mobile tank repair shops.

All of these are controlled by front authorities as a rule, but some may be attached to armies when necessary. Their operations are controlled from the front's rear control post by the deputy front commander for armament and equipment.

We first-observed this equipment in the early 1970s, stored in battalion-size sets of about 40 items of equipment. The number of these sets has nearly doubled in the last decade.

25X1

25X1

25X1
25X1
25X1

25X1

25X1

40

25X1

In the mid-1970s (according to their writings of that time) the Soviets were planning to increase the size of their front maintenance units from battalions to regiments, and around 1980 we began observing regiment-size equipment sets stored at armored vehicle, wheeled vehicle, and artillery maintenance facilities in East Germany. At engineer, missile, and signal repair facilities, however, the mobile maintenance equipment sets continue to reflect a battalion structure.

Both Soviets and East Germans staff the fixed maintenance facilities shown in figure 18. We have no firm evidence, however, to link these peacetime employees with most of the wartime mobile maintenance units represented by this mobile equipment

battalion-size nondivisional mobile maintenance units have been deployed in Afghanistan. Each usually can perform medium repair. The unit at Bagram, for example, was divided initially into three separate areas—for the repair of armored fighting vehicles, engineer equipment, and motor transport vehicles. Later, two additional maintenance areas were added for signals and electronics equipment and for artillery (figure 20).

What we observed at Bagram caused us to reconsider our estimates of the Soviets' potential to mobilize mobile maintenance units in East Germany. Initially, we had associated a mobile maintenance equipment set with the type of maintenance performed at the facility where it was stored. For example, we judged that the sets stored at the Wunsdorf tank repair plant would be used to equip mobilized field tank repair units. The activity observed at deployed mobile maintenance units in Afghanistan, however, demonstrated that such a unit probably can repair several types of equipment. Therefore, we no longer believe we can categorize the mobile maintenance equipment sets stored in East Germany by type of repair.

As for quantity, however, we believe the Soviets probably could mobilize more than 80 battalion-size mobile maintenance units in East Germany. This would be enough for at least two fronts.

These mobile units are only part of the maintenance formations available in East Germany. As noted in the section on Conventional Ammunition Stocks in East Germany, when divisions and armies depart for combat operations, their fixed garrison facilities are to be transferred to a higher echelon—at least to a front, if not to the TMO. Therefore, a front's maintenance base is to include some fixed maintenance facilities in addition to the mobile units whose equipment has been pre-positioned.

25X1

25X1

We also believe that in wartime at least some of the major fixed repair installations in East Germany are to be subordinate to the TMO. This is because some of these fixed facilities perform capital repair, and we know that a front is intended to have only a limited capability for capital repair in wartime.

25X1

25X1

25X1

Movement of Men and Materiel

According to their writings, the Soviets plan to deliver some 500,000 to 700,000 metric tons of supplies to their advancing armies during a front operation. They expect to ship most of this tonnage by rail or road, but they have plans that involve the integrated use of all forms of transport—rail, truck, air, and ship. The Soviets believe this integration is essential because lines of communication (LOCs) are likely to be disrupted in a nuclear war, and reliance on a single form of transport would jeopardize their logistics system.

25X1

25X1

The authors of articles published through 1980 indicate that within a front (or army) staff organization, the chief of a service (the Fuels Supply Service, for example) is responsible for maintaining stocks of critical supplies, but it is the deputy commander for rear services who plans and organizes all types of transportation.[29] His responsibility involves not only

---

[29] One exception to this split responsibility for maintaining stocks and for transporting them apparently occurs in the case of nuclear ammunition. The PRTBs and ORPDs (described in the section on nuclear ammunition) not only store missiles and warheads and deliver them to firing units but also have special transport equipment. In making deliveries, however, they undoubtedly must coordinate with the deputy commander for rear services, because he is responsible for controlling the flow of traffic on front (army) motor roads.

25X1
25X1

25X1

25X1

25X1

25X1

25X1

the delivery of supplies forward and the evacuation of casualties and damaged equipment to the rear, but also the maintenance of LOCs and the control of traffic within the rear area of his front (or army).

At either of these echelons the deputy commander for rear services is assisted by a transport services group. This includes personnel from the Military Transportation Service (*Voyennyye Soobshcheniya*, VOSO), the Road Troops (*Dorozhniye Voiska*, DV), and the Motor Transport Service (*Avtomobiliniye Voiska*,

AV). In wartime he is also assisted by an operations group from the Railroad Troops (*Zheleznodorozhniye Voiska*, ZhV); this ZhV group is located at the front or army rear control post. The actual storage and transport of supplies probably is handled by the front or army material support units.[30]

25X1

25X1

[30] See section on Organization of Rear Services.

25X1

25X1

Soviet authors indicate that transport assets can be managed in various ways:

- As a rule, a superior echelon uses its own means to deliver supplies to its subordinates. Thus, a front deputy commander for rear services might organize deliveries to army supply bases using trucks from one of his front's material support brigades.

- When necessary, however, he has the authority to use transport from subordinate echelons or to skip echelons for deliveries. He may, for example, order the use of trucks belonging to a subordinate army to deliver from a front supply base directly to a division.

- Finally, a front unit located deep in the rear (for example, a unit in the reserves, second-echelon forces, or rear services—which together consume about a third of the supplies used in a front operation) can deliver supplies "to themselves," using their own means of transport, leaving the front's transport means free for deliveries to advancing armies.

Rail Transport

Rail Networks
The East European nations have well-developed railroad networks (figure 21). According to a study prepared by the Defense Intelligence Agency (DIA), these railroads are the Warsaw Pact's primary means of long-haul ground transportation, and they are continually being improved, under various national programs, to increase their load-carrying capacity.[31] Four of these networks are particularly dense (table 4), and three of these (in Czechoslovakia, East Germany, and Poland) are opposite the NATO Central Region.

During peacetime the Soviet forces in Eastern Europe receive supplies via these non-Soviet Warsaw Pact national railroad systems.

the movement of all military trains was

[31] See DIA intelligence report DIA/DDB-2000-6-79 , August 1979, *Warsaw Pact Lines of Communication*

controlled by the appropriate regional operations directorate of the national railroad ministry. Trains had civilian engineers but were accompanied by military security detachments, and their progress was monitored by small military elements permanently stationed at civilian railroad control offices.

25X1
25X1

Military Rail Shipments in Wartime
Warsaw Pact military railroad capabilities probably are limited during peacetime, but they are to expand in wartime, using the civilian railroad industry as a base:

- there are four corps of Soviet Railroad Troops (administratively subordinate to the Ministry of Defense) that work on construction projects for the Ministry of Transport Construction in peacetime. During wartime, these are to expand to 16 corps and are to protect, restore, build, and operate railroads as part of a military force.[32]

25X1
25X1

25X1
25X1
25X1
25X1
25X1

- Warsaw Pact writings indicate that railroad personnel are to be mobilized for military operations during a war.

25X1
25X1
25X1
25X1
25X1
25X1
25X1

43

25X1

Figure 21
Railroads in East Germany, Poland, and Czechoslovakia

700804 (545416) 2-84

Soviet and Warsaw Pact writings indicate that during a war trains will be expected to handle 75 percent of all shipments from the deep rear as far forward a front's forward supply base. For this the authors specify that each front should have two or three axial railroads and two or three laterals, each line able to handle 60 to 70 trains per day in each direction.

According to the DIA, several rail lines in Eastern Europe can fulfill these requirements. Several of the routes in Poland and Czechoslovskia shown in figure 24 can handle 200 trains per day in each direction, and two of these enter East Germany—from Poland via Frankfurt and from Czechoslovakia near Dresden. Within East Germany, several major rail lines provide

25X1   25X1

44

25X1

axial and lateral connections along the inner-German border and within East Germany.

25X1

Motor Transport

Soviet writings indicate that during a war some 85 to 95 percent of all supplies that move from the front's forward supply base to the subordinate armies are to be shipped by motor transport. They specify that a front should have two or three motor transport brigades—that is, a capability to transport in one lift about 9,000 metric tons per subordinate army. Each army, in turn, should have a motor transport regiment capable of transporting 5,000 to 7,000 metric tons.

Motor Transport Units in East Germany
The Soviets plan to fulfill part of these wartime requirements with the equipment of several nondivisional motor transport units stationed in East Germany. Those units, subordinate to various front, army, and air force commands, are shown in figure 22 Altogether they can carry up to 66,000 metric tons in some 4,500 trucks and trailers.

- A front motor transport brigade housed at locations in Furstenwalde, Kummersdorf, and Luckenwalde. It is equipped with some 1,400 cargo and 660 POL trucks, which can transport up to 22,580 metric tons of cargo and 7,680 metric tons of POL.

- A motor transport regiment associated with a front artillery division. This unit, located at Potsdam and Karl-Marx-Stadt, is equipped with 420 cargo and 120 POL vehicles and can carry 5,880 metric tons of cargo and 1,200 metric tons of POL.

- Five motor transport regiments associated with armies in the GSFG. Each of these regiments has 120 to 180 cargo trucks and 60 POL trucks and can carry 2,100 to 2,800 metric tons of cargo and 600 metric tons of POL.

- Six motor transport battalions and one motor transport regiment associated with air forces of the GSFG. Altogether, these units can carry 7,140 metric tons of cargo and 5,160 metric tons of POL.

Table 4
Density of East European Rail Networks

25X1

	Density [a]
Bulgaria	38.7
Czechoslovakia	103.0
East Germany	132.0
Hungary	90.0
Poland	85.4
Romania	46.5

25X1
25X1

[a] The density figure shows the kilometers of rail lines per thousand square kilometers of territory. Data are for 1977.

25X1
25X1

During the late 1960s and early 1970s, the Soviets replaced older ZIL -and Gaz trucks (3.5 to 5 tons) in large motor transport units with Ural models of 5 to 7.5 tons. They paired each Ural with a 5-ton trailer to provide a lift capacity of at least 10 tons per vehicle. By the end of 1973, the Ural truck-plus-trailer was the primary vehicle observed in motor transport units of the GSFG. In the same improvement effort, the Soviets may have about doubled the amount of equipment in the GSFG front motor transport brigade to roughly its current number of trucks.

25X1
25X1
25X1

25X1

During the late 1970s the Soviets replaced the Ural truck-trailer combinations with new Kamaz models. The Kamaz 5320, a diesel-powered 6x4 cargo truck with a capacity of 8 tons, was introduced first. Each was accompanied by a two-axle 8-ton trailer, so each truck-trailer combination had a total capacity of 16 metric tons. The Kamaz 5320 was followed immediately by the Kamaz 5410, a 6x4 diesel-powered truck tractor that hauls a semitrailer with a capacity of at least 14 metric tons. This replacement of Urals with

25X1
25X1

25X1

25X1

Figure 22
Major Soviet Nondivisional Motor Transport Units in East Germany

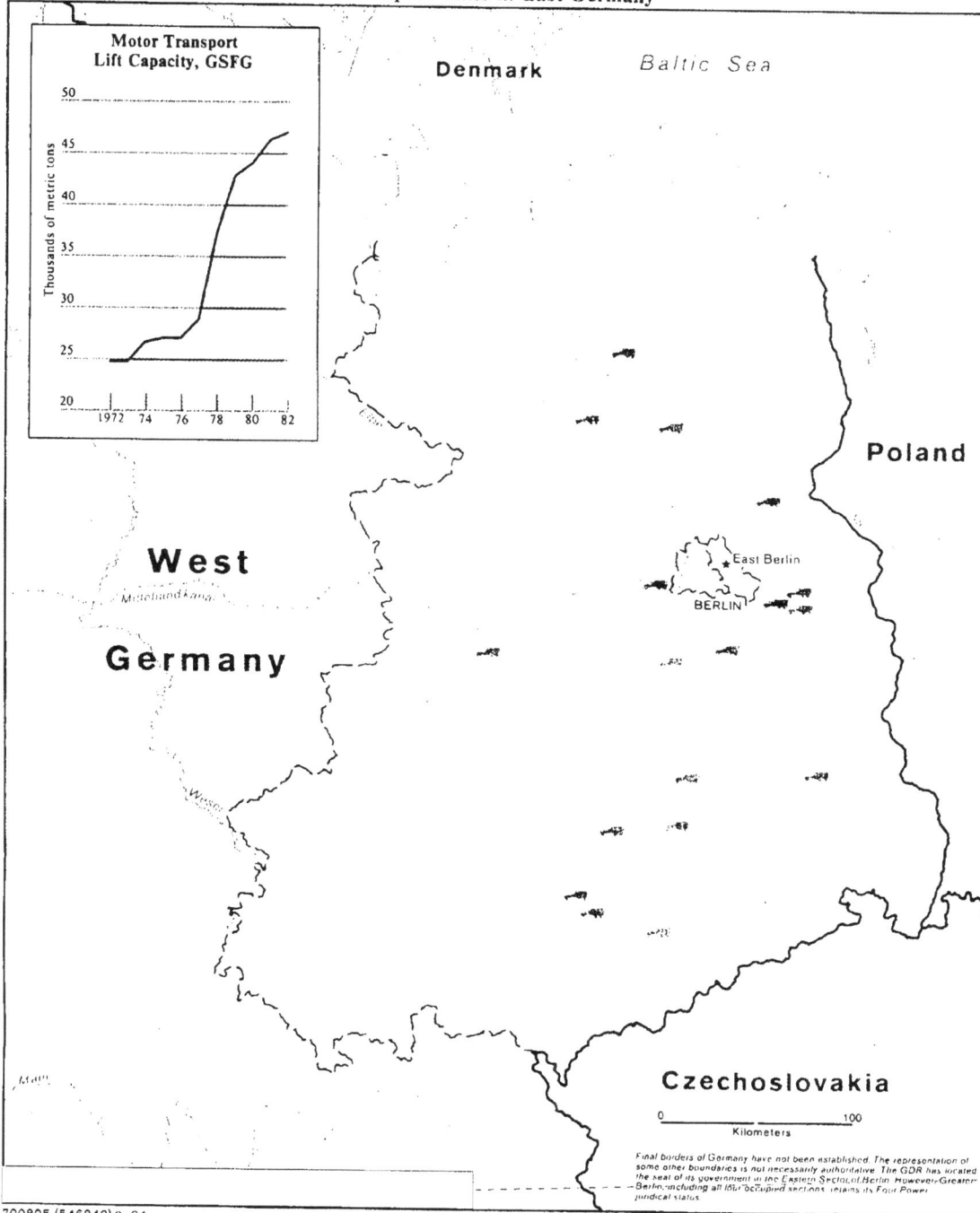

Motor Transport
Lift Capacity, GSFG

Denmark   Baltic Sea

Poland

West

Germany

East Berlin
BERLIN

Czechoslovakia

0   100
Kilometers

Final borders of Germany have not been established. The representation of
some other boundaries is not necessarily authoritative. The GDR has located
the seat of its government in the Eastern Sector of Berlin. However, Greater
Berlin, including all four occupied sections, retains its Four Power
juridical status.

700805 (546840) 2-84

25X1

46

25X1

Kamaz trucks increased the lift capacity of active front and army motor transport units by around 60 percent, with no corresponding requirement for additional drivers.

"Excess" Trucks Stored in East Germany

the Soviets have stored large numbers of additional trucks throughout East Germany. These trucks (sometimes called floats) may number 15,000 to 20,000, for a cargo capacity of some 60,000 to 80,000 metric tons.

At Dresden. A transshipment and distribution facility at Dresden has been operational since the 1960s. According to   analysis of satellite imagery, until about 1975 this facility stored trucks newly arrived in the GSFG, as well as older models awaiting shipment back to the Soviet Union. Since then, however, we have observed only new trucks at the Dresden facility.

According to satellite imagery, in the past three years as many as 500 Ural, ZIL, and Kamaz trucks have been at Dresden for extended periods of time awaiting distribution

At Rostock. Since 1977, a transshipment and distribution facility has been constructed at Rostock. Trucks are delivered to it by Soviet merchant ships, primarily by ships designed for roll-on/roll-off (RO/RO) operations. They are maintained in an equipment storage area until they are distributed. As many as 300 trucks are stored at any one time, most of them cargo trucks with capacities of 5 to 8 tons. All types of trucks are unloaded at Rostock, but most of those observed in the storage area are Kamaz, ZIL, and Ural military models

At Maintenance Facilities. In 1978 the Soviets began to store large numbers of trucks for extended periods at several of the major maintenance facilities of the GSFG.   many of these trucks are used for harvest support activities,

Each year the GSFG mobilizes 20 to 22 provisional motor transport battalions, sending personnel and at least 12,000 general purpose trucks and support vehicles back to the Soviet Union to assist with harvest activities.

Totals. The number of excess trucks in East Germany increased in the late 1970s

the number of trucks at Koenigs Wusterhausen had increased to about 1,600. Harvest markings on at least half of these vehicles were associated with 14 of the GSFG's annually mobilized transport battalions.

Age of the Soviet Truck Fleet in East Germany
Since the 1970s the Soviets have not only increased the number and lift capacity of trucks in East Germany but also regularly replaced trucks with newer models. Currently the active motor transport units there have a cargo truck fleet that is five to seven years old. This regular renewal, combined with the Soviet maintenance and conservation practices, probably assures the military that its trucks are reliable.

Estimates based on analysis of satellite imagery indicate that since 1975 the number of older model or obsolete trucks leaving East Germany for harvest support has been greater than the number returning.

25X1

47

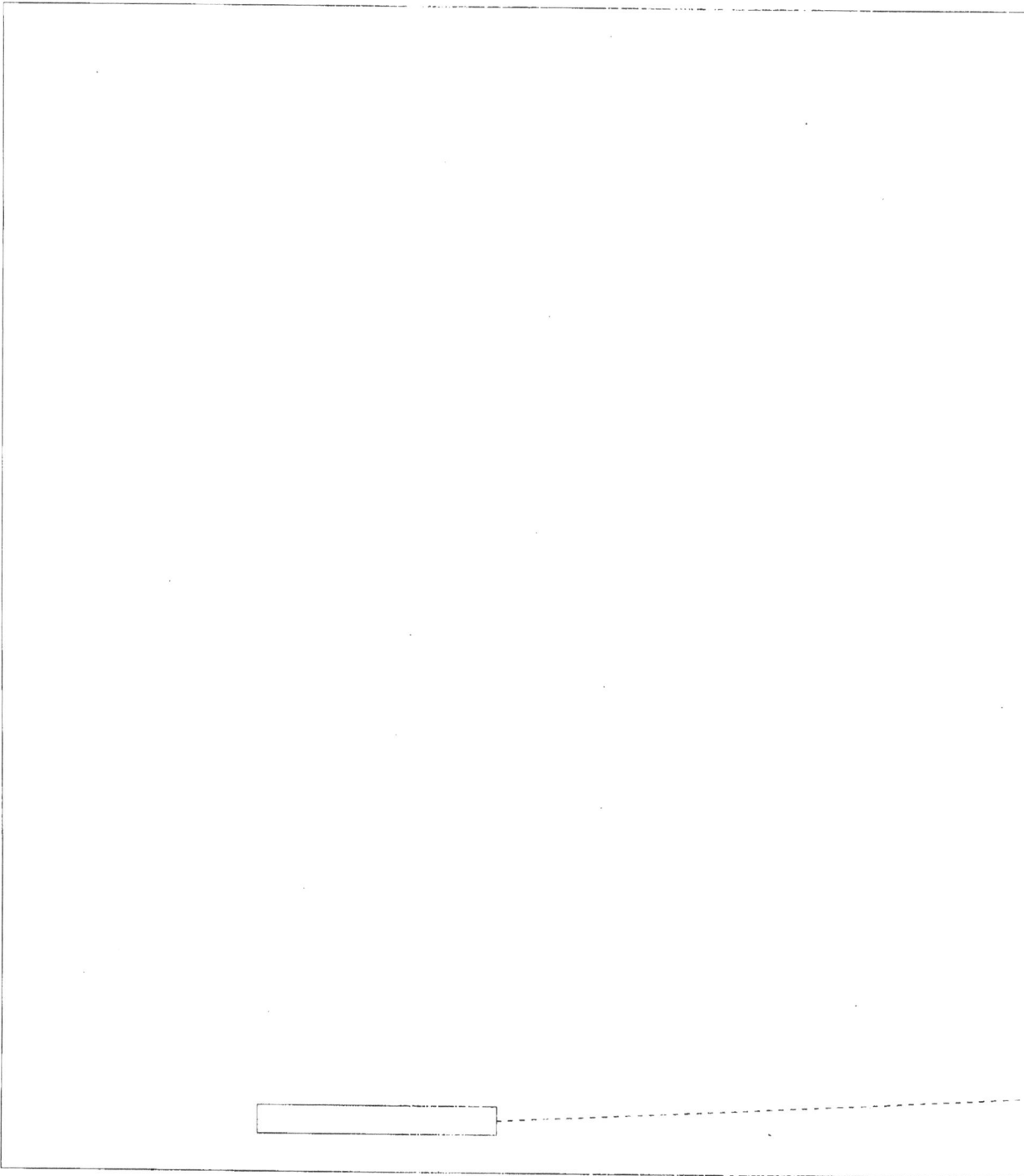

25X1

25X1

HR70-14

25X1

25X1

in or who were familiar with harvest support activity in the GSFG, cargo trucks that had high odometer readings or needed repair were selected for harvest duty and administratively removed from unit accountability records. After the harvest some of them were sold, usually to collective farms in the USSR. The ones shipped back to East Germany were either serviced and reissued to units or replaced by new trucks. ⎯⎯⎯⎯⎯⎯⎯ 25X1

This use of the harvest support cycle as a means of refurbishing the Soviet truck fleet is apparent in the overall makeup of the harvest vehicle fleet. According to ⎯⎯⎯⎯⎯ 25X1

- During the late 1960s and early 1970s the newer Ural 375 was replacing the ZIL-157 and Gaz trucks as the primary motor transport means of the GSFG.
- Through 1977 the GSFG sent out harvest fleets consisting almost exclusively of ZIL and Gaz trucks.
- Fewer ZIL models (especially the obsolete 5-ton ZIL-157) returned to the GSFG.
- In 1977 the Kamaz truck began to be introduced into the GSFG.
- By 1980 the Urals composed about 25 percent of the harvest fleet and the ZIL-157s only about 23 percent—more than 50 percent less than in 1977.

Ural 375 trucks were first observed in the harvest fleet in 1977 and Kamaz trucks in 1980. We believe that whenever a truck of a newer model was drawn for harvest duty it probably had seen service in the portion of the Soviet truck fleet that is used frequently. ⎯⎯⎯⎯⎯⎯⎯⎯⎯⎯⎯ 25X1

Few Soviet vehicles are used regularly in peacetime. Activity patterns noted on satellite imagery suggest that only 10 to 15 percent of any unit's vehicles are driven frequently and that the rest are in storage except during large training exercises. The Soviets have a strict maintenance regimen for those vehicles in their transport fleet that are stored for long periods. Their writings indicate that these vehicles are to be inspected regularly and deficiencies corrected at a maintenance facility. The Soviet conservation practices are almost identical to some of those used to preserve vehicles in the US POMCUS (pre-positioned overseas materiel configured in unit sets) stored in

West Germany. The practices undoubtedly are intended to maintain the Soviet fleet in factory condition for as long as possible. ⎯⎯⎯⎯⎯ 25X1

Traffic Management

Soviet authorities realize that movements on a scale permitted by the large number of trucks in East Germany certainly would be chaotic without some form of organization and control. At each echelon, the deputy commander for rear services is responsible for movements on motor roads in the area of his command. To assist him on the roadways themselves, the Soviets provide traffic control troops and an organized system of military motor roads. ⎯⎯⎯⎯⎯ 25X1

Road Requirements

Specific military motor roads have been designated for specific fronts and armies. Soviet writings indicate that within the zone of a front, one main road and one auxiliary road are prepared for each subordinate army. Overall there might be three or four main and three or four auxiliary roads. Within an army zone, one motor road is prepared for each subordinate division. ⎯⎯⎯⎯⎯ 25X1

Soviet estimates of the requirements for these roads have increased. In the late 1960s Soviet writings indicated that the capacity of front motor roads was to be some 4,000 to 6,000 vehicles per day on main roads and 2,000 to 4,000 on auxiliary roads. Army roads were to sustain movement by 1,000 to 2,000 vehicles per day. By the mid-1970s the Soviet estimates of front road requirements had increased to 8,000 to 10,000 vehicles per day, but army road requirements remained unchanged. ⎯⎯⎯⎯⎯ 25X1

To fulfill these requirements, Eastern Europe has an efficient system of highways and autobahns (figure 24). DIA estimates that these roads can handle the volume of military traffic the Soviets anticipate for wartime. ⎯⎯⎯⎯⎯ 25X1

25X1

Figure 24
Highways in East Germany, Poland, and Czechoslovakia

700806 (545416) 2-84

Traffic Control

Soviet writings indicate that plans exist for establishing traffic control areas and sectors to organize the flow of traffic on military roads in wartime. Within each area and sector, traffic control troops are to direct the flow of military traffic, report on the progress of convoys, relay instructions to convoy officers, report the condition of the roads, and monitor for signs of nuclear or chemical contamination. These troops will assist convoys by establishing areas for medical aid, vehicle maintenance assistance, food and fuel, and—when necessary—rest and warming up.

25X1

50

25X1

In order to do this, according to Soviet authors, a front should have three or four traffic control brigades. Each brigade is to establish some 25 dispatcher points, 160 traffic control posts, three servicing points, and nine medical aid points. These points are to be set up along front and army motor roads so as to ensure continuous control over the movement of military convoys. They can be augmented if necessary by motorized rifle troops from second-echelon units.

We judge that traffic control units are inactive in peacetime and that their functions are performed by motorized rifle troops detailed as needed to direct traffic along convoy routes. Warsaw Pact writings indicate that traffic control units are among those to be mobilized. In Poland, for example, traffic control personnel are to be provided by the Ministry of the Interior.

Maintaining Lines of Communication

Since the mid-1960s Soviet authors have expressed concern that during a war the LOCs would be vulnerable to attack—especially fixed structures like bridges. Destruction of a bridge could prevent traffic from crossing a major obstacle. To maintain an uninterrupted movement, they advocated preparing march routes in advance, providing for the restoration of damaged road segments, and constructing bypasses around major railroad junctions and industrial centers.

Just as restoration of damaged railroads is to be the task of railroad troops, road repair is to be the task of road troops. Soviet authors indicate that civilian organizations are to be used as much as possible for road repairs.

Their locations suggest that the parts are intended to replace bridges along major LOCs that may be damaged in combat. The design of the bridges in these stockpiles indicates that 28 are East German—reflecting the predominant role of the host nation in providing for the maintenance of LOCs.

The Soviets have also stored reserves of lighter tactical bridge and assault crossing equipment throughout East Germany. (These reserves are over and above the bridge sets found in tactical units.) The sites of the stockpiles for both fixed and ponton bridges are shown in figure 25

Construction projects by civilian ministries frequently reflect military priorities. Consequently, we believe that continuing improvements to East European roads and railroads probably reflect, at least in part, military plans for development of transport means in time of war.

Conclusions

Our analysis indicates that the Soviets intend to have ample logistic support for fighting a war. They plan to consume massive amounts of supplies and to reconstitute the forces of a front or of a theater of military operations as much as possible with its own resources. The significant aspect of the Soviet logistic system is that most of this support is found not at the tactical but at the operational (that is, front and army) command level.

We believe the implications of the Soviets' preparations are far reaching and can be appreciated only when they are considered in the aggregate. This consideration can involve both the geographic locations of their logistic formations and means and the extent of their material preparations.

Locations of Logistic Formations and Means

Soviet logistic bases are located throughout East Germany. Most of them, however, are south of Berlin (figure 26). This focus of logistic preparations suggests that Soviet wartime operations probably will emanate from the western and southwestern areas of East Germany.

51

25X1

Figure 25
Reserve Bridging Equipment in East Germany

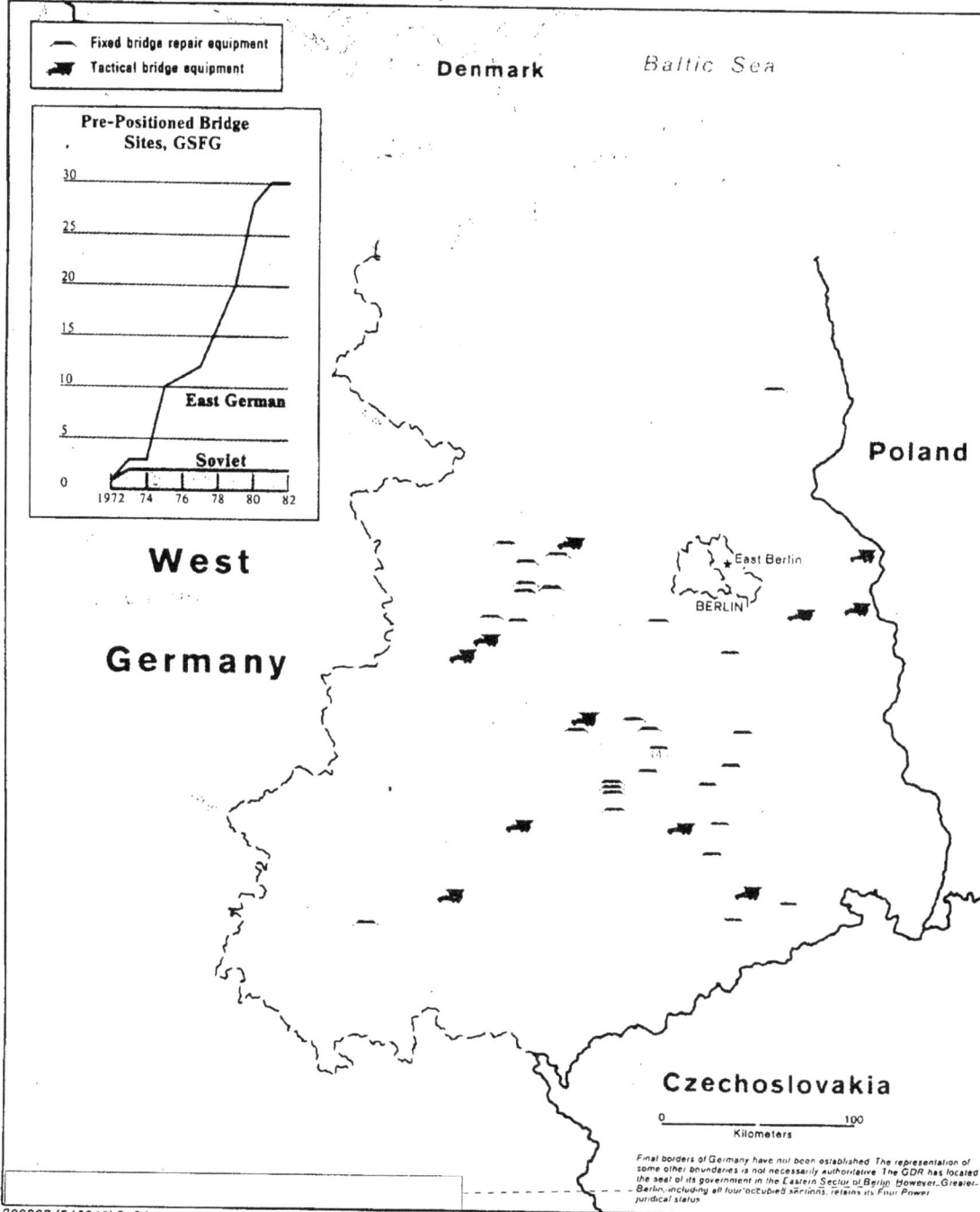

Legend:
— Fixed bridge repair equipment
🚚 Tactical bridge equipment

Pre-Positioned Bridge Sites, GSFG
(East German / Soviet, 1972–82)

Denmark · Baltic Sea · West Germany · Berlin · East Berlin · Poland · Czechoslovakia

Kilometers 0–100

Final borders of Germany have not been established. The representation of some other boundaries is not necessarily authoritative. The GDR has located the seat of its government in the Eastern Sector of Berlin. However, Greater Berlin, including all four occupied sections, retains its Four Power juridical status.

700807 (546840) 2-84

52

25X1

We have located some Soviet logistic installations north of Berlin, but not nearly as many as in the south. From this we conclude that Warsaw Pact units operating in the north are more likely to be non-Soviet than Soviet forces, and at present we cannot estimate the extent of the NSWP logistic preparedness. 25X1

The logistic support structure that we observe in East Germany appears to be compressed during peacetime. We judge that at the beginning of a war the combat formations are to be supported by the materials and personnel already in place at fixed installations. As the troops advance into central and southern West Germany (and farther from these facilities), however, the Soviets will deploy mobile field logistic units behind the combat echelons. These probably will be manned by reservists, according to timetables and requirements established in peacetime, and deployed by front commanders where they are most needed. In developing this logistic network, the Soviets have anticipated a need to support combat operations ultimately to a distance of 800 to 1,000 km 25X1

Plans for Front and Theater Logistics

The location of the logistic facilities also suggests that they are arranged to support more than a single front—perhaps the TMO. We base this judgment on several considerations:

- Soviet writings indicate that a *forward front supply base* is to be located "near the national boundary" and that POL is to be delivered to such a base by pipeline. The arrangement of pipelines and tactical field pipe stacks in East Germany suggests strongly that forward front supply bases could be established at three places—near Magdeburg, Erfurt, and Gera.

  — Soviet writings also indicate that a front might have one or two forward supply bases. The establishment of three such bases in this area suggests that the Soviets may be preparing the logistic base of the Western TMO in East Germany.

- *Major storage areas for ammunition and POL* are located about 100 to 150 kilometers from the West German border. *Divisional storage areas* are located much closer to the border, in areas that might be likely positions for at least portions of forward front supply bases. Because all fixed installations become the property of the front when divisions and armies move out of them, it is possible that these division storage areas are to form front supply bases and that the major storage areas in the rear are to form TMO reserves. 25X1 25X1

- *Soviet hospitals* are distributed throughout East Germany more evenly than any of the other types of logistic facilities. They are accessible from the northern, western, and southwestern areas of East Germany.

- *Capital and medium repair maintenance facilities* are located in two major clusters—one around and to the west of Berlin, and another in the Leipzig–Dresden–Karl-Marx-Stadt area. All are accessible from major lines of communication, which provide access to any of the major potential combat zones. It is possible that the facilities in the south might support a Soviet front in the west or southwest, while those around Berlin might repair vehicles evacuated from throughout the TMO. 25X1

- There is a plethora of high-capacity *lines of communication* connecting the length and breadth of the country, and all pass through the central region (including the Berlin area). If, as we judge, supply bases in east and central East Germany are part of TMO reserves, they could deliver supplies along these LOCs to the northern, western, and southwestern parts of East Germany—where wartime fronts are likely to originate.

- *Soviet truck parks* are located throughout East Germany, in locations that could serve as bases for the support of operations in any of the major combat areas. 25X1

25X1

Figure 26
Focus of Soviet Logistic Preparations in East Germany, 1982

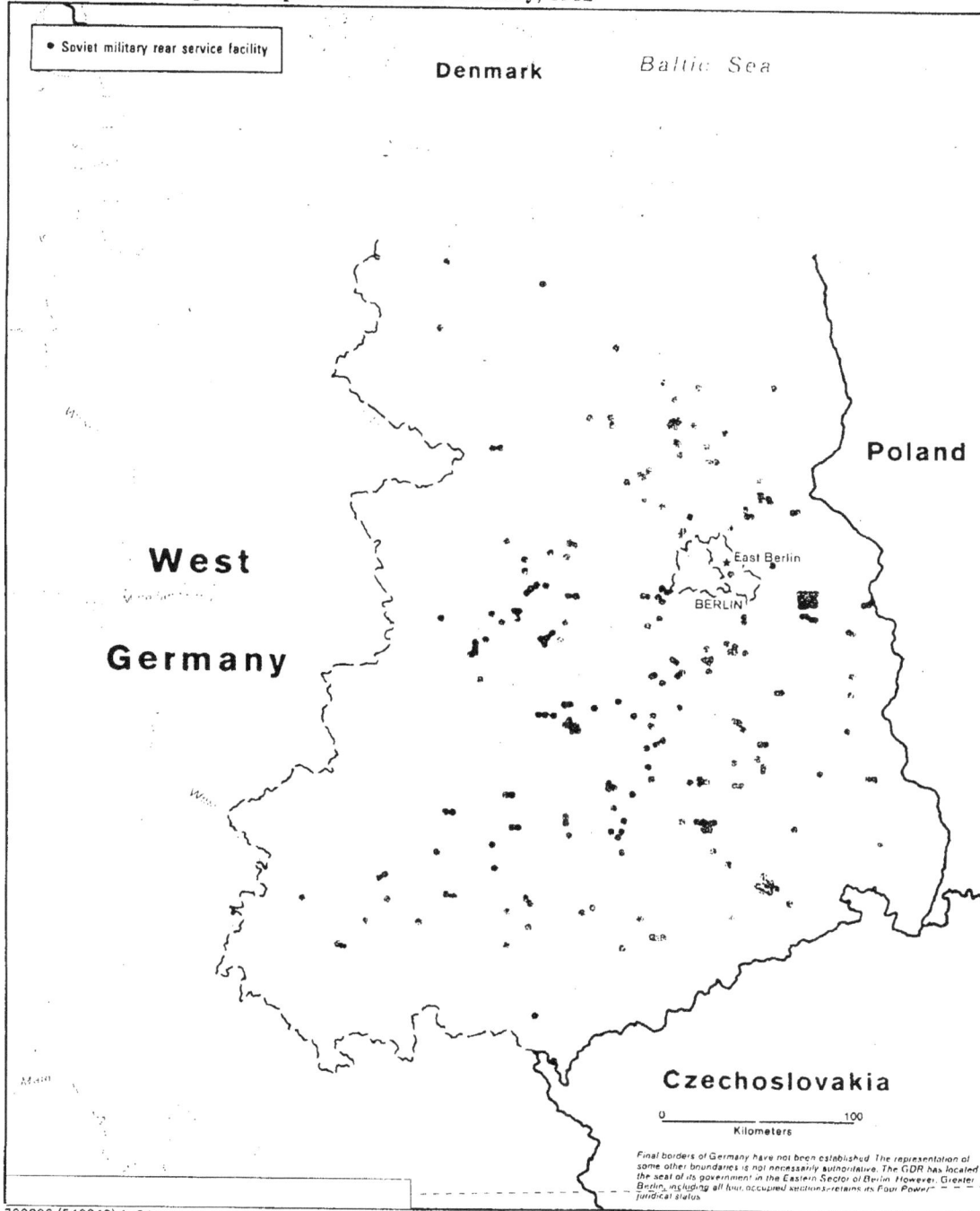

- Soviet military rear service facility

Denmark

Baltic Sea

Poland

West

Germany

East Berlin

BERLIN

Czechoslovakia

0   100
Kilometers

Final borders of Germany have not been established. The representation of
some other boundaries is not necessarily authoritative. The GDR has located
the seat of its government in the Eastern Sector of Berlin. However, Greater
Berlin, including all four occupied sections, retains its Four Power
juridical status.

25X1

700806 (546840) 1-84

54

25X1

Extent of Material Preparations

A further appreciation of the extent of Soviet logistic preparations in East Germany can be gained from a consideration of the general Soviet norms for a front and the degree to which the material preparations and medical or maintenance capacities fulfill those requirements. It should be noted that no effort has been made to validate the Soviet norms by any kind of gaming or modeling. The comments below indicate our view of the extent to which the Soviets have met their own norms:

• Fixed *ammunition storage* facilities in East Germany have enough capacity to store more than 500,000 metric tons of ammunition. This is enough to satisfy Soviet requirements for about four front operations or peacetime war reserve stockpiles for about two fronts. (We cannot determine the mix of ammunition stored in these areas, so some—especially the newer—types of ammunition could be in short supply.)

— Ammunition storage capacity at front and army depots has about doubled since 1977.

• The Soviets' military *POL storage* areas alone have the capacity to hold more than 500,000 metric tons—enough to satisfy their requirements for about two front operations or peacetime stockpiles for one front. When these stocks are augmented by fuel contained in main pipelines or in East German national reserves committed to the TMO, they enable the Soviets to fulfill their norms of POL for at least one front, and probably more, using reserves stored in East Germany.

• According to their norms, the Soviets probably have enough hospital beds in their *military hospitals* in East Germany to treat casualties from about two front operations. We believe that some garrisons vacated by first-echelon combat formations are likely to be used as additional hospitals and that the East Germans are required to provide an undetermined number of hospital beds for the TMO. In this case, the military medical establishment in East Germany almost certainly is capable of satisfying Soviet medical requirements for at least two fronts.

— Since 1970 the amount of equipment pre-positioned in East Germany for mobile medical units has nearly doubled.

• The Soviets have developed an extensive capability to repair and rebuild military equipment at *fixed maintenance installations* in East Germany. Consequently, they do not find it necessary to remove damaged equipment out of the TMO for repair.

— The Soviets also pre-position equipment for mobile maintenance units. The amount of this equipment has doubled in the past decade and is now adequate to satisfy their norms for at least two fronts.

• The *lift capacity* of the Soviets' military trucks in East Germany far exceeds their requirements for a single front. These probably are to be supplemented by East German military transport units and by trucks mobilized from the East German economy; with such additions, the Soviets could comfortably meet the requirements for two fronts. 25X1

The presence of these logistic facilities and stockpiles does not necessarily mean the Soviets could fight a prolonged war in their present configuration. They are probably confident, however, that they could sustain the initial period of a war. We believe the Soviets have established enough stocks and capabilities to support their concept of combat operations for a short period, using their logistic manpower and materials already in East Germany. For extended operations they would have to mobilize large numbers of personnel to fill logistic formations. These personnel could be transported into East Germany by air and rail transport mechanisms that are already in regular use for the semiannual troop rotations. 25X1

25X1

Finally, the Soviets have steadily expanded their logistic capabilities in East Germany during the past decade. We estimate, for example, that the capacity of their ammunition and fuel depots has nearly doubled since 1977, that equipment pre-positioned in peacetime for wartime mobile medical and maintenance units has doubled since the early 1970s, and that the lift capacity of active nondivisional motor transport units has increased by around 60 percent through the introduction of the Kamaz trucks since 1978. Indeed, for every aspect of logistics that we considered—even those for which we were unable to derive rigorous data—we have noted expansion or development since the early 1970s.

Taken together, these observations indicate to us that during the past decade the Soviets have methodically improved their capability to support their forces in East Germany to such an extent that logistic buildups, which once might have been key indicators of impending military operations in Europe, now probably have little potential to provide such warning. Ten years ago the Soviets probably doubted that they could support a war in Europe with supplies stocked there; to do so would have required amassing materiel from the USSR. Now, however, we see every indication that logistic preparations in East Germany so completely fulfill their doctrinal norms that the Soviets probably feel confident they can support at least the initial period of a war using materiel pre-positioned in East Germany where they believe it is most likely to be needed.

This shift could also portend Soviet capabilities to reinforce the forces in East Germany sooner than before. In the past, Soviet supply convoys (part of a logistic buildup) probably would have clogged roads across Poland during mobilization and the early period of a war. Because logistic stocks have been pre-positioned in East Germany, however, we suspect that the Soviets now have the option of moving combat formations almost immediately, if necessary. Even though they might choose to move some supplies across Poland to replenish pre-positioned stocks, it seems likely that formations made up primarily of combat units could move to Central Europe as soon as they could be dispatched from the western USSR.

25X1

25X1

25X1

25X1

25X1

Appendix A

Theoretical Considerations of Soviet Artillery Fire Planning

Planning requirements for ammunition, inventories of requirements for operations, and expected consumption rates are calculated in terms of a unit called a *boyevoy komplekt* or *boyekomplekt* (BK). Soviet authors indicate that when the concept of a BK was introduced, long before the 20th century, it referred to the ammunition consumed in a single day of intense combat. By the turn of the century, however, the BK had come to refer to the supply of ammunition both at the guns and in the limbers and cartridge boxes of an artillery battery.

25X1

As weapons became more advanced, the term evolved and became more general, until now it is little more than a supply calculation unit. Thus, according to the Soviet *Dictionary of Rocket and Artillery Terminology* (1968), a BK is:

> . . . a quantity of ammunition, established for a unit of armament (gun, mortar, machinegun, submachinegun, propelled gun, armored transport, and other).

> A boyevoy komplekt serves as a supply calculation unit for computing provisions and requirements of subunits (units) for ammunition necessary for the fulfillment of a certain military problem. The size of a boyevoy komplekt is different for each form of armament.

Each individual weapon has a specific BK. Normally, a rocket launcher (with multiple launch tubes) has a BK of three salvos, while a tank, self-propelled gun, or other vehicle-mounted weapon has a BK equal to the ammunition storage capacity aboard the vehicle (table 5). The BKs of other weapons are based on the characteristics and functions of the weapon, combat experience, and the transportation available.

In most cases, the number of rounds in a BK appears to be an arbitrary multiple of 20, possibly so that certain planning calculations can be carried out easily. Calculations with BKs normally involve the weight of the BK in metric tons because this is important in

Table 5 Examples of Boyekomplekts	*Rounds* (except where noted)
Weapon	BK
152-mm howitzer and gun-howitzer	60
122-mm howitzer and 130-mm gun	80
100-mm gun	100
Multiple rocket launcher	3 salvos
240-mm mortar	40
160-mm mortar	60
120-mm mortar	80

25X1

25X1

transport planning, but for certain computations volume is also calculated. These weight and volume figures can then be used—in connection with other standardized measurements, such as the POL refill and the daily food ration—for planning transport or storage needs.

25X1

A military organization also has its overall BK. This is the total of the weapon BK or BKs multiplied by the number of similar weapons in the unit. Thus, a battalion may be said to have "1.5 BKs on hand" or to require "3.5 BKs for a coming period of operations."

25X1
25X1

Finally, the BK may be standard or special. Standard BKs include a normal mix of ammunition types. For 122-mm howitzers, for example, a BK might be made up of 90 percent high-explosive rounds, 5 percent antitank rounds, and 5 percent smoke, illumination, chemical, or self-destructing rounds. A unit may ask for a special mix of ammunition for a specific mission.

25X1

A standard BK may not include newer types of ammunition, which thus require special requisition and allocation.

25X1

25X1

25X1

All Soviet and Warsaw Pact fire planning is done in terms of the BK. In addition, according to written NSWP doctrine, the allocation of ammunition for an operation requires consideration of both operational-tactical and organizational-technical factors.[33]

25X1

Operational-tactical considerations include:

- *The type of operation.* Ammunition consumption is likely to be much higher during offensive operations than during defensive ones and higher during conventional than during nuclear warfare.

- *The strength of enemy forces and their method of operation.* The stronger the enemy and the better prepared his defenses, the greater will be the amount of ammunition required.

- *The strength of friendly forces and the types of weapons with which they are equipped.* The availability of nuclear weapons—including tactical ground-based weapons, air-launched weapons, and strategic weapons available to support an operation—can reduce the amount of conventional ammunition required.

- *The ratio of friendly to enemy forces.* If this ratio favors the attacker, ammunition expenditures probably will be less.

- *The expected duration of the operation.* The longer the operation, the more ammunition it will require.

- *The effect of terrain.* If the terrain favors a well-entrenched defender, an attack will require a greater amount of ammunition.

Organizational-technical considerations include:

- *Available supply rates.* Artillery commanders have norms that tell them how much ammunition should be available for their units, but these norms can be adjusted to correspond to a tactical situation—or to the amount of ammunition actually available.

[33] NSWP countries use training manuals written by the Soviets, and we believe that the NSWP doctrine we are examining here probably applies to Soviet forces as well.

- *Fire effectiveness indexes of shells of the various calibers.* To simplify planning, the fire effectiveness of every weapon is expressed in terms of a common index, the M-38 122-mm howitzer. For the BK of a single-projectile, this index is expressed as a ratio of the number of projectiles for the basic gun to the number of projectiles required to neutralize concealed weapons and personnel on one hectare of surface area. For the BK of a gun (weapon), the index is expressed as the ratio of the number of projectiles to the number of projectiles in a BK of the index weapon multiplied by an established projectile conversion coefficient.

  25X1
  25X1

  — Artillery planners probably use these ratios to develop alternative targeting strategies and to determine the weight and volume of ammunition they will need, so as to plan the transportation of ammunition to firing units.

- *Principles for the use of artillery.* Published norms specify the number of rounds usually required for weapons of different calibers to destroy or neutralize a given target. (For example, the norm might allocate 220 rounds of 122-mm ammunition to neutralize an artillery battery 10 kilometers distant.)

  — Other norms are established for the commitment of artillery units to battle. A divisional artillery unit, for example, always supports its division (or that division's subordinate regiments), and an army artillery unit supports the divisions subordinate to that army. Reinforcing artillery units generally are attached to first-echelon divisions to provide greater fire support during an offensive.

25X1

25X1